Nowhere to Go but Up

Gavin C. Solomon

Copyright © 2012 Gavin Solomon

All rights reserved.

DEDICATION & ACKNOLEDGEMENTS

To my beloved parents for supporting me in chasing my dreams and

for putting up with this pain in the ass

To all the dreamers who believe in working hard and never giving up

To all the people who doubted me, look at me now

I wasn't born with a passion for business. My passion for business stemmed from my goal of obviously making money but more importantly my love for solving problems. Business is just one problem after another and when something is starting to seem like it's going smoothly a new unexpected problem will arise. I started off investing my spare change into penny stocks and eventually blue-chip stocks. After I built a portfolio I took my gains and invested it into bitcoin and other cryptocurrencies. At that point, I had a decent collection of cash so I decided I wanted to take it to the next level. I ended up brainstorming ideas for my next venture and I realized there is one market that will never die…medical supplies and equipment. It was like a lightbulb went off in my brain. There will always be a high demand for it regardless of the state of the economy or the consumer. I found a niche and I developed a strategy and executed it. I filed for incorporation in Febuary of 2015 doing business as The Medical Supply Guy. I'm still young and have so much more to learn but even with that being said, I have accomplished more then some adults have but not because I had better opportunity, because I never gave up on my dreams and wouldn't let anyone hinder my success. Anyone can be successful if they have grit and an indefatigable itch for accomplishing their goals. My business has had a lot of good periods and bad periods and we have succeeded and failed. It was a learning experience for me and I developed a passion for it. I am young and eager to learn. I went in charging like a bull and came out flying like an eagle. I look forward to failing because it allows me to better myself and my business for the future. Even when I'm a loser, I'm a winner!

1

LISTEN UP

None of us are born a successful entrepreneur. We all come into the world in the same way namely naked, scared and ignorant. What then separates us are the choices we make during our lives. These choices can range from whether we go into further education, who we marry, the career we choose, living a healthy life and the list goes on.

Making the right choices are important as ultimately these choices will determine how successful and happy we will become in life. Even when we make the wrong choice, many of us fear changing that decision as we fear taking the necessary action to make our lives better.

This applies to those who have made bad career choices. Many will continue to complain that they hate their job which then impacts on their home life, but most will still not take the necessary steps to change their lives for the better.

Even those who are brave enough to take action and start their own business sometimes still make the wrong choices that will still lead to failure and dissatisfaction. So, what separates the successful entrepreneurs from the amateur entrepreneurs?

Both sets of entrepreneurs are focused on becoming successful and both work hard to achieve their goals. However successful entrepreneurs are aware that success will not happen overnight and they build their success slowly and consistently and avoid the common pitfalls faced by their less successful counterparts.

Some of the downfalls that many entrepreneurs experience include:

<u>Slow and Steady Wins The Race</u>

Successful entrepreneurs realise that success will not happen overnight. They acknowledge that even seemingly small steps will eventually lead to the peak of the mountain. Like the story of the tortoise and the hare their goal is about adopting positive behaviour and habits and above all being consistent until slowly, but surely, they go on to win the race. They realise that in order to become successful they will need to work very hard to achieve that success. They also do not become complacent when they have achieved success. Instead they continue to do the things that have made them successful realising that consistency is key to long term success.

Self Education

Self education in another major reason why some entrepreneurs are more successful than others. Technology is constantly changing and therefore for any kind of entrepreneurship, educating yourself in the evolving environment is paramount to success especially for those who have online businesses.

Take 100% ownership

To become a successful entrepreneur accountability is a must. You will need to take full responsibility for the way that your business is run. Amateur entrepreneurs have the tendency to blame any shortcomings on bad luck or on other people. However, any mistakes made are, again, as a result of making bad decisions. For example if mistakes are made in a script that has been written for you it is wrong to blame the scriptwriter, as ultimately you should have taken ownership and checked the script before the presentation. Likewise it is your own fault and not bad luck, if you overstretch yourself financially and then factors go against you. A good businessman would make a better decision by allowing for any eventualities that might happen and keep a reserve of cash in case.

Time Management

Don't waste time doing things that don't need doing. One of the biggest flaws that many entrepreneurs make is trying to do everything themselves. It is important to manage your time wisely and only the things that you need to do.

Learn From Other Successful Entrepreneurs

This is the most important difference between a successful and an amateur entrepreneur. It is far easier to become successful by being guided by other successful individuals who have been down that path before you. Even famous entrepreneurs have been influenced by other successful people. Richard Branson was advised by Freddie Laker before venturing with his airline and Steve Jobs was inspired by Robert Noyce of Intel.

It is far better to avoid costly mistakes by listening to the more experienced experts. A good mentor will not only teach you how to become successful but they will also let you tap into their own network, allowing you to surround yourself and learn from other successful people.

They will teach you the leadership and behaviour that you need to adopt to become successful.

There are many online communities that will offer mentorship programs by top business experts. The advantage of joining a reputable community is that you will have access to tools, training, focused education and live coaching calls that will equip you with all you need to know make the shift from amateur to successful entrepreneur. With technology and marketing constantly changing it can be hugely advantageous to have access to the most up to date methods that have been tried and tested by someone else's money rather than your own. All you need to do is to implement what you are taught one step at a time.

Having mentoring and coaching, in my opinion, is paramount to succeeding especially with an online business. In any business, entrepreneurship skills are crucial to becoming successful. Therefore you will need to learn the necessary skill sets required to become successful.

Being mentored by another business entrepreneur can help to steer you on the right path to becoming a successful entrepreneur.

So, one might ask why I'm giving this adivise and what qualifies me to do so. Well, I may be young but I have accomplished more then a lot of adults but not because I had better opportunity but rather I don't let anyone get in the way of my success and I have one thing most people lack which is drive. If you have drive and have your mind set on your goal then you're on your way to greatness. Nothing can stop you unless you let it.

I never had any idea that I would end up doing what I do. How many people can say they ended up doing what they thought they would. I can assure you there isn't too many. No one knows for sure what they will do tomorrow but what they do today determines all of their tomorrows. I never thought I would be running a medical supply business while I'm in high school but I am and I love every second of it. Of course, it is a balancing act and very time consuming and stressful but I reap an extrodinary reward and I'm not talking about money. The reward I get is the satisfaction of knowing I'm not sitting around waiting for something to happen like most people my age are. I'm setting myself up to have a secure financial future and piece of mind knowing that I have a job that I am passionate about and great at. I figured that I can either work for an entrepreneur or I can become one. I always knew I wasn't meant to be like everyone else. Since I could remember I knew I was destined to do something great with myself because I have confidence in my abilities and everyone should. Everyone should think they are born to be great and no one should settle for less. We are put on this Earth to help it not to mooch off it. No one should expect to be given something if they don't work hard for it. Everyone has the ability to be something but hardly anyone has the ability to stay the path and keep going even though they fail time and time again. You must have drive to succeed and there is nothing complicated about it. I have failed too many times to count and I have barely scratched the ceiling. Most people quit after failing but what does that accomplish? If you fail then use it as motivation to do better next time. Don't see failure as a negative experience rather see it as a positive experience that you learned from. Everyone falls down but only a few get back up.

2

THE MIND SET OF THE SUCCESSFUL ENTREPRENEUR

What sets apart a successful entrepreneur from people who are not successful, whether in their own small business, or in a job? Looking externally, the entrepreneur is a normal, everyday person just like everyone else - they need to eat, have a roof over their head, they have obligations, to themselves, their families, their communities.

They have their own idiosyncrasies, fears and challenges too, just like everyone. Yet, somehow they have taken their energy, resources and talents and produced something extraordinary - a business which adds value to society, is profitable, and with those businesses and their lives are leading a life of purpose, profits and passion.

Putting a regular person next to the successful entrepreneur, at first glance, you would not be able to tell them apart. Yet these two proverbial examples would be doing drastically different things which lead them to significantly different results. To find the reason, we will have to look at the root cause of their actions, which is the mindset.

The mindset of a person encompasses several different things - how he views and defines this life of ours on Earth, his purpose, his self, his beliefs and his values. It is this mindset of the person which defines how he views or interprets what is going on around him, and how he gives them meaning. It is the meaning of these events and his situations that will determine his emotional state and thus the decisions he makes. These decisions will in turn determine his actions, and his results.

It is because the results of the successful entrepreneur and the ordinary man are so different, that we can attribute the root cause of it to be the difference in mindset. So what makes the mindset of the successful entrepreneur different?

Owning Your Own Destiny

First and foremost, the successful entrepreneur does not attribute the reason for his success or failure on luck, other people, the government, the economy. He may or may not believe in the presence of a divine being, or the one-ness of the universe, but regardless lives by the saying 'If it is to be, it is up to me.'

In other words, the first step to being successful is that of owning your own life and fate. Know what is within your control, such as your emotions, your actions, the people that you associate with, and your attitude. Successful people bulldoze past bad luck, obstacles, naysayers, fears and risks through believing that whatever they envision, they can make happen with the right approach and perseverance.

Vision

One common trait found in successful people is that they have a strong vision for what they want to achieve. For example, Bill Gates' vision when he started Microsoft was that every household would have a personal computer. He believed in the positive life-changing force that computers represented and developed a strong and motivating personal vision for it. It is described that this big vision pulls the entrepreneur towards it, rather than him having to push tiresomely.

Doing Whatever It Takes

The successful entrepreneur also commits to doing whatever it takes to making his vision come true. This is the definition of commitment and truly what makes them succeed, for most people run at the first sight of blood. The moment something goes wrong, they say, "That's it, this is not the right thing for me. I knew that it wouldn't work anyway." Successful entrepreneurs know that their success, or at least their next level of success, lies behind the obstacle that lies just behind them.

How many stories of successful entrepreneurs have you heard, where the entrepreneur loses his house, his car, his relationships, in order to see through his business? The lessons from these stories are not proverbial. In your journey as an entrepreneur you will be challenged, and there will be times where you will have to make very difficult choices, to either push on to do whatever it takes, or to give up. In order to succeed, you have to see things through, and that requires doing whatever it takes. You should be relentless in your pursuit of success and under no circumstances let someone or something change your mind.

Being Decisive and Taking Action

Richard Branson famously said "I can make any decision within 60 seconds." Being an entrepreneur, time is never on your side.

Technology, consumer tastes, competition move fast and if you don't keep up, you may face being in the wrong place at the wrong time, and failing in your venture. In order to move fast and stay ahead of the market, you will have to not only have a keen eye for trends and what is to come, but you will have to be decisive.

Most people balk at the idea of the heavy responsibility of making an important decision. The weight of peoples' expectations - partners, clients, employees, family and friends, can be unnerving. Successful entrepreneurs take decisions in their stride, one at a time, and do what is best, even if it is difficult.

Continuous Improvement and Humility

One key question entrepreneurs ask themselves all the time is "How can I make this better?" They constantly ask this about the world around them, the systems they interact with, the products and services they use, and most of all, their own being, when it comes to work and life. Many people might think that being successful, wealthy and famous, a successful entrepreneur would be allowed to say "Well, that's it. I've learnt all I need to learn."

Counter-intuitively, it is really the nature of humility and continuous improvement that drives successful entrepreneurs to where they are.

When Jack Welch, the renown ex-CEO of General Electric, was asked what he looked for in any candidate, he said "The first thing I look for is candor." Candor is the attribute of being frank, in giving opinions, feedback, and going about work. This is what the successful entrepreneur looks for, people who surround him that continually give frank and constructive feedback, always challenging him to make things better.

Contribution

Last but not least, the successful entrepreneur is driven by a sense of contribution. They understand that they exist as part of a larger community and as an inhabitant of the world we live in. In order to make life better for everyone, each one of us has to play a part and contribute. It is with this understanding that successful entrepreneurs examine the world as it is, and identify what problems exist and how they can make things better.

It is with this drive that these entrepreneurs are able to get out of bed with energy to do the extraordinary things that they do. If you are driven solely by a selfish reason of financial reward or the image of drinking cocktails on a beach, then it is likely that one day, when you're feeling challenged, tired or demotivated, you would tell yourself "I don't need this money. I don't need these challenges. I don't need the cocktails." and simply stop. Think about what your contribution, your legacy, in this life is.

There are many things which you cannot control in business; the market environment, your competitors, financial markets; realise that in just a moment, you can change your mindset to one that supports you towards your success. Adopt a successful entrepreneur mindset and see the change in your business and your life.

3

CHARACTERISTICS OF SUCCESSFUL ENTREPRENEURS... DO YOU HAVE THEM?

Most people are longing to start their own businesses. But do they know what it takes to become successful entrepreneurs? What about you? Which characteristics of successful entrepreneurs do you bring in the business you have or you intend to begin? Before going any further into the details, let me define an entrepreneur as someone, who makes money by starting businesses with some kind of financial risk-taking involved. Is that what you are?

Well, every person joins business with various reasons. These reasons usually determine the performance of the business. I have discovered that many people think that success in business depends upon being highly educated, having lots of money and a supportive family. However, the bottom line of success in your business is motivation, fuelled by the desire to achieve and the enthusiasm to do your business. A highly motivated person tends to behave in a certain way that leads to success and it's a distinguishing factor of all successful entrepreneurs. How motivated are you?

Through this article, allow me to share with you 15 characteristics of successful entrepreneurs that are fundamental to building a successful business. If you are aiming at succeeding in your business, then it's high time you started acquiring the following behaviors…

1. **BE AN INNOVATOR**. To succeed you have to be creative. All successful entrepreneurs think a lot differently from ordinary people. They see things other people have not yet mirrored and are able to introduce new things and new ways of doing things.

2. **LEARN TO SOLVE PEOPLE'S PROBLEMS.** Successful entrepreneurs are problem solvers. They have the ability to identify specific problems of a given customer group, which require their products or services to be solved. As they solve their customers'

problems, they end up making money. Turning people's problems into great opportunities is one of the characteristics of successful entrepreneurs.

3. **BE AN INFORMATION SEEKER.** There is no successful entrepreneur who is not hungry for knowledge. You have to get new knowledge, new information and new skills for you to become successful in what you are doing.

4. **PERSISTENCE WILL HELP YOU TO SUCCEED.** All successful entrepreneurs keep on and on no matter how hard the going may be. They are success-conscious and believe in succeeding despite all roadblocks. They believe that riches come only to those who work hard and long. Indeed! By working hard and consistently long, riches begin to power so quickly and in such a great abundance that you even wonder where they have been hiding during all those years of toiling.

5. **LEARN TO SET GOALS.** This helps them to know where they are going and how to go there systematically. Without setting goals you are like someone who is blindfolded and asked to shoot the target. You will never know where the target is and you will only be gambling.

6. **COMMITMENT TO WORK.** How committed are you to your work? Successful entrepreneurs are able to initiate and to pursue their work contracts to the end. They are self-driven and do not need anybody to drive them, to supervise them.

7. **DEMAND FOR EFFICIENCY AND QUALITY.** Demanding for efficiency and quality is one of the characteristics of successful entrepreneurs. They detest mediocrity and can never settle for that. They are able to achieve the desired results without wasting their energy. They always aim at offering goods and services of the highest quality.

8. **BE HARD WORKING.** Successful entrepreneurs are hardworking people. They spend a lot of time, energy and other resources working on their businesses to achieve the desired results. They expect to get what they expect. They think big and strategically.

9. **AIM AT ACHIEVING YOUR GOALS AND DESIRES.** All successful entrepreneurs are achievers. They do not give up when faced with a temporary defeat. They do not despair because they are highly motivated people. Whatever they put their hands and their minds on, they commit themselves to achieve it. Until they achieve it, they do not stop. Even after achieving it, they look forward to

strengthen their achievements.

10. **BE A RISK TAKER.** Taking moderate risks is another characteristic of successful entrepreneurs. They don't fear to take risks. FEAR to take risks discourages initiative, brings about uncertainty of purpose, destroys ambition, kills enthusiasm, destroys good reasoning and stops you from taking action. Besides, there is nothing you can engage yourself in without any risks involved.

For instance, by just driving your car to go to work, you risk getting involved in an accident. But if you already know it, you take precautionary measures to avoid getting an accident other than opting not to drive. That's how successful entrepreneurs go about their business. They anticipate the risks involved and think of how to overcome them in case they manifested.

11. **DESIRE TO BE INDEPENDENT.** Desiring to become independent is one of the characteristics of successful entrepreneurs. They have a strong drive to be masters of their own life, to take their own decisions and to pursue their own destiny.

12. **LEARN TO CONTROL YOUR OWN DESTINY.** Successful entrepreneurs control their own destiny. They don't lose focus of what they pursue. Having a strong desire to walk their road

to riches is one of the characteristics of successful entrepreneurs. The end justifies the means.

13. **BE DETERMINED.** Successful entrepreneurs are so strong-minded that they do not give up despite any obstacles. They are always determined to transform their desires and thoughts into their monetary equivalent at any cost.

14. **HAVE SELF-CONFIDENCE.** Successful entrepreneurs don't depend on luck. They are able to visualize and they believe in the attainment of their desires at all cost. Ability to visualize and to have faith in the attainment of your desires is an important factor in building your self-confidence.

Developing a high level of self-confidence is a key element in effective business management and success. You need to be sure of yourself to tackle the tasks at hand. You need to have high expectations of achieving success. If you think you can, then you can. But if you think you can't, the chances are that you cannot. "Yes, we can", is the winning formula President Obama applied to become president. You, too, can follow the same principle to become a successful entrepreneur.

4

10 ATTRIBUTES OF SUCCESSFUL ENTREPRENEURS

Do you ever wonder what it is that makes one entrepreneur very successful and another not? Is it luck, timing, money, connections, intelligence, honesty, dishonesty, attitude or that it is just meant to be for some and not for others? I have put together a list of 10 attributes that are universal for all who wish to be successful entrepreneurs. Successful does not mean being Dale Carnegie, Bill Gates, Donald Trump or Mark Zuckerberg. It means achieving the success you want in your life. This is not my opinion but attributes taken from other lists over the years as well as from the many books I have read that have discussed the keys to success for many successful entrepreneurs.

1. **Creative Thought** - It is the creative thought of the entrepreneur that inspires them to go forth and make a difference. For each of us

as entrepreneurs, creativity will never be lacking. In fact, too much creativity may be our biggest downfall. Too many times we get caught up in the excitement of the creative idea that we lose focus on the most important task at hand. Creativity is the lifeblood of the entrepreneur. Almost all we have today is because an entrepreneur came up with the idea for change or betterment to what currently existed.

2. **Courage** - Despite all the odds we know are against us we go forward with our desire for entrepreneurship. Courage is the knowing the risks that you must face, yet going forward with your desire for your new entrepreneurial venture. Think of the world with no personal computers. Imagine they do not exist. Let's say you've heard of these things called computers, but they were really for the big secretive companies, government and maybe very, very rich people. Now imagine a guy coming up to you and saying that he was going to invent a computer that would be called the Personal Computer and that in a short time every household would have at least one. How crazy would you think this person is? That is not exactly how it happened but close enough for our discussion here. Because of that crazy idea with all the odds against him Bill Gates had the courage to

go forward and today is the second richest man in the world, with a net worth of $56 Billion.

3. **Bravery** - In the midst of start-up or business growth the entrepreneur does not think of who this is for, why it is worth it or the consequences of failure. They push forward with the fortitude of success. Bravery is different from Courage in terms of action. Bravery is the act of "the fight" and not caring how big the odds are against you. But Bravery exists because of the desire to win and you put it all on the line. Successful entrepreneurs have both courage and bravery. They have the knowing of what is against them and as they enter the ring of battle they put all to the side and focus on success. Their bravery comes from a deeper place, not that just of money but of success for a personal and deep emotional reason. If they do not have a deep emotional connection to the reason for their success their bravery is empty and will not succeed.

4. **Confidence** - The entrepreneur has a "knowing" that they can achieve their dream. No matter what anyone else says to them, Confidence is not blissful ignorance. Confidence means that after acquiring the research, data and facts needed, knowing that YOU can make it work. A high level of confidence is extremely important

because there will be many things that will happen during your pursuit of success that will challenge your belief and of those around you. Did you know that Colonel Sanders, of Kentucky Fried Chicken, went to 1009 restaurants (which took over 2 years) before he received his first yes. 1009....how many of us would have kept going after 50...100...200...not me. I would have thought I had a bad idea and gone back to rethink. Not him. He had confidence in his idea and was not going to let anything or anyone break that confidence. God bless him.

5. **Humility** - To balance their confidence the successful entrepreneur needs to know that they don't have all the answers. Although confident, they are humble enough to understand that they must always be open to the feedback of the world around them and be willing to absorb, analyze and decide which feedback will help them to achieve their dream. Stubbornness is just stupidity with an attitude. If there is one thing the successful entrepreneur is not, is stupid.

6. **Learner** - It is at that moment that you feel you are "there" that you are then the furthest you have ever been from being there. The entrepreneur must be the perpetual and hungry student. The longer

we are in business, the more experience we gain, the more knowledge we accumulate, the more we realize how little we know. Learning is the key to succeeding.

7. **Strategist** - Very, very few businesses become successful by chance. Successful entrepreneurship takes thought, planning, execution, analysis, evaluation, adjustments and implementation. In a word, Strategy. Imagine you have been dropped in the desert with 2 days of water and 3 days in every direction but one, until you reach a water supply. If you guess which way to go, you are more than likely dead. However, if you take time to strategize where you are now and which direction is the most likely path to water in two days not three, you have greatly upped your chances of success. The strategist is all about working smart not hard. The strategist understands the muscle between your two ears is much more powerful than all the other muscles in your body, combined!

8. **Focus** - This is the myopic thought process of success. If you know what you want and you stay focused on achieving "that" then all you do will continue to get you closer to achievement. As mentioned above, creativity is usually the one attribute of the entrepreneur that can make them never reach success. Non-focused

creativity can cause us to put time and energy into things that are not of the most immediate importance. Staying focused is the key to clear and productive creative thinking.

9. **Determined Perseverance** - The successful entrepreneur is determined to succeed no matter what gets in their way. You will have tough times. You will want to quit. You will be frustrated, tired, exhausted, depressed and stressed out. It is okay. Just persevere. Your determination will drive your perseverance. It is said that Thomas Edison had at least 10,000 failed experiments until he came up with the right formula for the electronic light bulb. Ten-thousand. That is a lot. Is there anything you would stick with if you failed at it 10,000 times? Now that is Determined Perseverance. Excuse me while I go shut off the light.

10. **Celebrator** - The hard-working entrepreneur knows when to celebrate. Encouragement for the entrepreneur rarely comes from the outside. Most of the "at-a-boys" have to come from each of us to ourselves. It is important that we celebrate our successes. We work hard for successes, but we must understand that we don't achieve success like winning the lottery. Our ultimate vision of success doesn't happen all at one time. It come in bits and pieces. Like

stepping-stones. There have been those few that do reach it at once, but they are few and far between. Most of them who succeed so quickly fail almost as quickly, because they have not been able to learn from the experience of failures. We must celebrate the mini-successes we have. The benchmarks of success are what let us know that we are reaching our ultimate goal. Otherwise the ultimate success we are looking to achieve may be too far off to appreciate.

These ten attributes of the successful entrepreneur do not stand-alone. You cannot have some without the others. Entrepreneurs are made up of many different types of people. Educated and non-educated, experienced and brand new, men and women, as well as, all races, religions and those of different socio-economic status. Anyone can be a successful entrepreneur if they continually develop their attributes. These are not in place of skills. This list is stating the foundational attributes needed. Communications skills, financial skills, leadership skills and the many others that entrepreneurs possess are not universal. These above are universal. We all need them in order to be a true entrepreneurial succes

5

SUCCESSFUL ENTREPRENEURS LIVE EXAMINES INCOME PRODUCING ACTIVITIES

Every successful entrepreneur who makes thousands per day, does it by engaging in income producing activities. This is the only way you can make money on the internet. Everyone that follows a daily routine of taking action to engage in income producing activities, will make money for their efforts.

The following is a list of 5 income producing activities that will make you money:

1.) Prospecting New leads

2.) Building Relationships

3.) Follow Up

4.) Online Webinars

5.) Public Sales Seminars.

Prospecting New Leads

Successful entrepreneurs all over the world prospect leads using various methods utilized on a daily basis. One method is emailing every lead on your list daily with new content you're creating for them to use in their businesses. Make sure you're creating content they can actually use right away. If your new content solves what ever agitation they are having with their business, you will establish trust with them and they will buy from you.

Another method is to post ads on Google and Facebook. This is probably the most popular and easiest way to obtain new leads and raise brand awareness. You can set your budget to a little as five dollars a day all the way to as much as you want. The great thing about this is you are practically guaranteed hits to your website and your phones should be blowing up if you do it right. You must set the parameters correctly to target your ideal customer or else your money is going in the garbage.

Building Relationship

By building relationships, successful entrepreneurs have turned thousands of leads into dollars. They create relationships through social marketing done on sites such as Facebook, Twitter, LinkIn, Pinterest, Share just to name a few. Many have made relationships though marketing forums such as Warrior.com, or moneymakergroup.com. Here they comment to other internet marketer's questions in an effort to solve whatever their problem may be. Every successful entrepreneur knows that as soon as he or she solves the problem in question, there is a good chance that the person, will buy from them. Now with credibility established, so do sales for the successful entrepreneur. Talking with people face to face about their problems making money online, and coming up with a solution to that problem, has also proven to be a very good strategy to turn leads into conversions.

Follow Up

Successful entrepreneurs always follow up with their leads to start the process of building the relationship between themselves and their new prospects. They utilize their leverage by following up on a daily basis by emailing or calling them on the phone. They know credibility cannot be established without first reaching out to say hello, thank you, or just for the purpose of introducing themselves to let their new prospects know that they are important and valued. No money has ever been made in this business without first following up with the people you are trying to turn into conversions.

Online Webinars

Successful entrepreneurs, no matter who they are or how they began, use online webinars as an effective method for creating leads and conversions all at the same time. Any new prospect that signs up for the webinar becomes a new lead instantly. If the subject matter in the webinar answers the problems the new lead is experiencing, he or she will buy from them turning their new lead into conversions for the successful entrepreneur. Either way, 100s of new leads can be created and turned into conversions using this method. In addition, this method is highly recommended by successful entrepreneurs worldwide.

Public Sales Seminars

Now this method is one of the most effective income producing activities a successful entrepreneurs will do. First, they will rent a public venue, like an auditorium or room easily accessible to the public, usually at a downtown location. In this room will be lots of seating, a good PA system, and a very successful entrepreneur who is a man with a mission. He is here to educate you about how he or she is going to solve your financial problem with the product they will be selling after the 1-2-hour speech or sales pitch.

The successful entrepreneur will not sound like they are giving a sales pitch, but like a solution to the people's agitation about the problem they are having in their online business. This builds a bridge of trust between themselves and their new client who will now be inclined to buy whatever product they are selling.

This also results in them being liked and admired, which will funnel into more downline sales of pipeline money for the successful entrepreneur. So, it is no surprise that the smart, motivated, and driven that take this kind of massive action, that success and riches soon follow these people where ever they go to market their products.

 Ultimately you can have a game changing product but it doesn't mean anything if you don't raise awareness for it by marketing to protential customers. The only way to do that is to follow in the footsteps of every other successful product out there and create a marketing campaign that will make your name echo in the customers head so they say "hey, I want to buy that."

Well, I hope you have gained some value and an understanding of what successful entrepreneurs do on a daily basis to become top earners in their prospective fields. And if your new and want to become a successful entrepreneur, you will take these lessons seriously and take massive action to create leads, create conversions, and change lives.

6

HOW SUCCESSFUL ENTREPRENEURS CREATE PROFITABLE BUSINESSES ONLINE AND OFFLINE

To succeed as successful entrepreneurs it takes 90% mindset and only 10% fundamentals. You need to understand the basic concepts of what you are trying to master but in order to stay in the game and remain focused it requires a different set of skills that needs to be practiced consistently. Anyone can start up a business with the right capital, but to create profitable businesses you have to properly learn how to market yourself to others while maintaining a positive mindset. A winner's mindset is focused on doing whatever it takes to get the business successful and out of all the people who decide to start an online business only a fraction of those individuals understand this principle. The first thing we will go over is how successful entrepreneurs interpret opportunities and handle conflicts of interest.

Assume Everything's an Opportunity to Make Money

Starting profitable businesses isn't an easy task, but if we understand how successful entrepreneurs think than we can understand the simplicity behind it. Entrepreneurs analyze every situation in a way that allows them to benefit in the end. Whether it's studying market patterns or buying furniture an entrepreneur finds a way to have that asset make him money. Starting profitable businesses requires a huge amount of energy to think outside of the box. Since most companies adopt a business model which is unique from other competitors, it's imperative that successful entrepreneurs think of new ways to have their money work for them instead of traditional ways of working for money.

Remove All Personal Limitations

The internet is one example of how many successful entrepreneurs have created profitable businesses online at extremely low costs.

Hence the word businesses, when dealing with the online world there are many opportunities for us to earn extra income. Successful entrepreneurs never settle for just one business. Why should you have only one successful business when you have the power and ability to own multiple. This mindset of endless possibilities dominates an entrepreneur and this clear distinction is what the majority of our population needs to understand. Most of society creates limitations for themselves by listening to their negative mind chatter. It isn't the start-up costs required for profitable businesses that determines it's success, but it's more of the decisions behind the person starting up the business and how he interprets different situations.

View Failure as a Learning Experience

If we want to truly succeed we have to look at failure in a completely new way. If every entrepreneur viewed failure as a statement defining themselves, then no one would be successful today. The key about successful entrepreneurs is that they find any negative situation and turn it into a positive. By learning from each failure they are stronger in the end and know what to avoid in order to obtain success. Starting profitable businesses takes huge amounts of failure in order to differentiate what works and what doesn't so in the future you are more prepared for what to expect and how to handle it. I look forward to failing and even when I'm a loser, I'm a winner aswell.

Utilize all your Resources

To create a profitable business we first have to think about what resources we have readily available to us which can generate us some profit. When we truly analyze our life situation we can discover mounts of resources at our disposal. The second thing to pay attention for are products, services, or ideas that people see value in purchasing. Bottom line if you have nothing that offers value to anyone, no matter how hard you work you will never make any money. Successful entrepreneurs find different growing trends within the market and pursue those trends until they have mastered the fundamentals behind it and have devised a strategy for how they can use it to make money. A perfect example of a growing trend right now would be the internet and work from home jobs. Nowadays different individuals are creating profitable businesses and offering work to many others at the same time. Most of these individuals didn't start off as successful entrepreneurs but they learned what they needed to learn in order to succeed in their field or trend.

Target your Market

Using the power and resources of the internet many people have found different ways to search and buy what they're looking for with just a click of a mouse. How successful entrepreneurs analyze this situation is by asking themselves "What services and products can I target that has a high demand and low competitors online?" This simple question can raise many possibilities for a new product to join the booming internet world and create constant residual profits. The internet has opened up a completely new industry in our economy that offers digital services and products for websites online and many internet moguls have made billions from selling things such as a plug in for website programs, anti-virus software, etc. you get the idea.

Effectively Manage your Profits

Profitable businesses can be started up from anywhere but once we create just one highly valued business that has the potential to generate us constant flow of residual income the opportunities are endless. That residual income can be used in whatever way you choose, but successful entrepreneurs find ways of having their hard earned money work for them. Choosing to spend is great of course, but sacrificing pleasure and practicing discipline is another highly valued trait most successful entrepreneurs have. Using the money earned from one business to start up another business or to invest is how most people double their money in just a few years. Creating profitable businesses is not an easy task, although it is fairly simple if you master and practice these concepts daily. Taking advantage of growing new trends can help as a leverage in creating your new business. Just think 20 years from now what will the internet be and how many people will still be using it? Part of being successful entrepreneurs isn't just seeing what's in front of us but analyzing what is ahead of us as well. Learn to work hard now and play plenty later!!

7

Aquire These Traits

Before you begin down the path of an entrepreneur you should take the time to ask yourself if you have or are willing to possess these 8 traits of successful entrepreneurs.

Work: As an entrepreneur you have decided to take complete responsibility for your financial future. Congratulations, are you now ready to put in the work? Yes, work! While the work we perform is typically a bunch of simple actions repeated over and over, we tend to work each & everyday. Most individuals in these professions love what we do so it's difficult to draw the line between work and play. Don't be shocked if you hear of us taking 3 day weekend because we definitely have the flexibility to do so however as a network marketing professional you will learn that people are our business. A simple work related email can be sent out Friday morning that generates hundreds to thousands of dollars over the weekend or by simply enjoying your weekend activities, you might come across some ideal prospects for your business and engage in some simple networking activities. The way I like to see it is like this; As an entrepreneur, life is my business and life is open 24/7/365. I can only get out of my business what I put in and it beats the 9-5 any day of the year.

Share: Zig Ziglar said, "You can have whatever you want in life if you help enough people get what they want". Therefore share your wisdom, skills and passion for life and the floodgates of abundance will open for you.

Manage: We all have the same amount of time to work with each day but what separates the successful individuals from those that fail is their ability to manage their activities in each day. Being that network marketing professionals work with people, it is also very important to be capable of managing people - their expectations and more.

Invest: Invest in yourself & other people who prove they are worth your valuable time. They way I see it, you are going to pay to learn a lesson either with much emotional turmoil & financial drain as you learn through your own experience or you can pay much less financially & avoid the emotional turmoil by investing in books, audio programs, workshops and more to learn from people who are currently experiencing what you want to experience. Don't view the currency you spend on training materials & workshops as an added cost but rather as an investment into yourself. Your business will only grow to the extent to which you are willing to grow as an individual.

Hunt: Hunters eat & the hunted get eaten. If you are not actively hunting & seeking new ways to live the life of your dreams then you are sitting prey to outside circumstances such as market fluctuations. However, this does not mean you hunt down your prospect and attack them with your business presentation every chance you get. With proper target marketing, you will not need to use this ineffective technique. Remmber that in the business world another one's loss is your gain.

Coachable: This is a tough one for many people because the EGO wants to believe that it knows everything it needs to survive. However, I'm not wanting you to be able to survive, I want you to thrive. We've learned to survive since the days of saber-tooth tigers and if you're reading this chances are you know how to keep a roof over your head and food in your stomach. Being coachable is keeping an open mind and being able to welcome positive criticism. It someone is taking the time to coach you then they believe you have the ability to thrive, so open up to their knowledge, implement what they share and be prepared to soar with the eagles.

Mastermind: We've heard the saying that two heads are better than one, well imagine a group of minds that are focused on success. You can definitely get ahead of the pack if your mind is absorbing the combined energy of the mastermind group. All it takes is one thought to transform a life.

Association: The quality of your relationships, your income level and every other area of your life is an average of the 5 people you spend most of your time with. You heard it before, "Birds of the same feather flock together", well it rings true for us humans too. So take a look at your contact list in your phone and even your Facebook friends lists and delete the negative people in your life.

More Personality Traits Most Successful Entrepreneurs Possess:

When looking at many successful entrepreneurs most people see someone who seemingly through luck and/or good fortune was able to capitalize on a great idea. What most people do not see is what it takes for these people to position themselves for business success and it is often neither luck nor fortune. In many cases the successes these people enjoy result from thinking outside the box in terms of acceptable standards, beliefs or behavior. Their ability to develop and act upon innovative ideas is what sets them apart and makes them successful. In many cases this ability can often be attributed to certain personality traits they possess and in fact may be traits that you possess as well!

Here is a look at what it is that allows some people to so easily develop and act upon innovative ideas while others may find doing so more difficult.

Risk Takers

Entrepreneurial success is usually experienced by people who are not afraid to take a chance with a new idea or concept. These folks are more daring than most and tend more of a 'what if' approach by following through on innovative ideas that others may shy away from. These people are not only thinking outside the box but they are also living there as well, and in most cases quite comfortably! They watch the crowd and go in the opposite direction because they know there will be less competition!

Defiant

Innovation is the key, in most cases, for business success however the majority are uncomfortable taking innovative measures. As a result they tend to criticize those who do take a 'different' path mostly because they are afraid others will succeed where they were afraid to even try! Due to these dynamics people who are not afraid of taking risks or trying something new learn to ignore criticism and are therefore viewed as more defiant. Ironically it is this defiance that is often responsible for many of the improvements those who criticize them may enjoy! The ideal entrepreneur will say 'screw the status quo' and will not take shit from anybody.

Self Sufficient

People who tend to be different from the majority, such as the novel thinking entrepreneurs we are discussing, have a much smaller base of support as a result. This in turn both calls for and requires them to be more self-sufficient as a result. Out of this comes the opportunity for them to further develop their resourcefulness which is not all too difficult considering their knack for thinking outside the box in the first place. Obviously a deep inner drive and belief in themselves needs to be existent! Are we perhaps describing you?

Successful entrepreneurs are viewed by many as people who found themselves in the right place at the right time. As true as this may be a closer look will reveal their uncanny ability to position themselves for business success by comfortably thinking outside the box and then acting upon it. In most cases this ability can be attributed to certain personality traits as discussed above. Folks like this demonstrate that the acceptable 'norm' is not always the right avenue to take for business success. Based upon their successes a common lesson we can all learn is that taking chances or being different is not always a bad thing!

Four More Traits for Success in Business

They are the driving force behind your business's ability to make money. They pay the bills. What are these four traits of success?

Attitude, Ambition Assertiveness and Action are the raw materials that make your business a success. Alone, however, any one or two of the four traits are generally insufficient to create a successful entrepreneur. Put together, the four traits are a force to reckon.

Attitude

Yes, you can program yourself to become a successful entrepreneur. You first begin with your attitude. Many of us undermine our chances for success by getting stuck in old negative thinking habits.

But the good news is that positive thinking habits are easily formed and once they are set in our minds we will find ourselves taking faster steps towards our goals and building success upon success in our business. Positive thinking helps you notice opportunities and seize them. Stay away from negative people for they are contagious. Nothing can pull you down faster than a person who tells you that, 'starting your own business is risky and you will go broke.'

Whenever you go against the grain, there is no shortage of people ready to put a spell or curse on your potential success. So an important step in getting what you want is consciously to surround yourself with people who are positive.

Ambition

Desire, Determination, Drive... Ambition. Do you have the burning desire to start your own business? Are you so hungry for it you can virtually taste it? Are you willing to place all your energy, willpower and effort behind your goal of becoming an entrepreneur? These are thought provoking questions you need to ask yourself to determine if you have the ambition to run your own business.

Assertiveness

Being assertive is essential for any entrepreneur to succeed in business. Assertiveness alone is like attitude or ambition alone and it is not enough. Many people are assertive but accomplish nothing. Guts without goals or guts without self-confidence usually lead to mean spirited entrepreneurs. However when assertiveness combines with ambition and a positive mental attitude a powerful trio exists and there emerges the entrepreneur with a can-do spirit, unwavering focus and the guts to tread where other tiptoe.

Action

Ask yourself, Am I a self-starter? Will I follow through on the steps I need to take to become an entrepreneur? Am I a person who can get results or I am just a talker?

All these questions have one aim: to find out if you are person of action. The most important trait an entrepreneur must have is the ability to take action. Having an excellent idea for your business is not enough. Millions of us toy with ideas. We toy but do not try, or we do not try long enough to get the payoff.

The entrepreneurs who live their dreams are those who stop considering all angles, weighing the pros and cons, and just go and do it. They understand that they can daydream about making more money, but if they are not willing to stick their necks out and set things in motion, becoming financially empowered through their own efforts is an elusive dream. They may not always be 'in the mood 'when they begin, but they do it anyway. They know that without action there is no change. Without change there is no excitement. Without excitement life becomes dull and monotonous and we become boring.

These traits are the prerequisites for success in your own business, but you do not need all of them in full supply before you begin. Right now, make up your mind to turn your idea into a business. Give your idea value by immediately acting on it. Regardless of how good the idea is, unless you do something with it you get absolutely nowhere.

Stop for a moment and take a good look in the mirror. Are you satisfied with your current position, occupation, schedule, financial status? If not think why you are in that position and what choices you have made in the past that got you to this place you are in today. Now think what factors gave light to these choices. Take these mistakes and learn from them to better yourself now and in the future. Anyone that is a success in business knows that they weren't always that successful and only got there by taking their experiences and mistakes and improving from there. Like the common saying "Rome wasn't built in a day" improving yourself isn't done in a day. Life isn't about finding yourself. Life is about creating yourself. Don't blame anyone but yourself because most commonly you are going to be your own worst enemy.

8

MINDSET TIPS TO BECOME A SUCCESSFUL ENTREPRENEUR

So why should you consider becoming an entrepreneur?

There are many reasons why you should consider taking that giant step and creating your own business.

Here are just a few of them:

1. **Autonomy** - Running your own business allows you to be in charge of your own destiny. It also helps you to avoid getting stuck in the "daily grind" or the "rat race". For many people running their own business lets them have a career that is self-sustaining.

2. **Opportunity** - Being an entrepreneur opens up a whole new world of opportunity for you. You will have the opportunity to do anything that you want in life. This means you can choose to spend your life changing the world for the better, or you can live the type of life you

want. Few other career choices can offer this kind of opportunity.

3. **Impact** - Many people who work for other companies truly want to work hard and help that company to succeed, but few are actually able to have such an impact. When you run your own business everything you do will directly impact the company, which can be very rewarding. You can either work for an entrepreneur or you can become one…the choice is yours.

4. **Freedom** - This is the answer most people will give if you ask them why they want to become an entrepreneur. For many people the idea of doing what they want and how they want to do is the most compelling reason to take the risk and run their own business. It is true- having freedom in life and career does make a huge difference!

5. **Responsibility** - When you run your own business you have the ability to be responsible to society and operate your business the way that you feel it should be run. This is especially true if you have the desire to help others or the world in general. If you work for someone else you may not be able to improve the world the way you want to, but if you are the boss you can.

6. **Being your Own Boss** - This is another common answer for why

many people want to become entrepreneurs. If you are your own boss you can do things your way. You can make your own decisions, take your own risks and decide your own fate.

7. **Time and Family** - Depending on your specific goals in life, becoming an entrepreneur could give you the freedom of time and allow you to spend more of it with your family.

8. **Creating a Legacy** - If the idea of forging a lasting legacy is important to you then few other careers give you the opportunity to do so like operating your own business.

9. **Accomplishment** - If you have specific goals that you would like to accomplish in your life running your own business could help you to do so.

10. **Control** - For a lot of business owners the sense of security that comes with the ability to control your own work is a major reason to become an entrepreneur.

So, you may ask what does it takes to become an entrepreneur?

There are plenty of benefits of being an entrepreneur, but it is certainly no easy task to start your own business.

Successful entrepreneurs, that is to say those who are able to accomplish their goals, earn a successful living through their business and enjoy the many benefits of entrepreneurship, all have specific traits.

If you are considering taking the leap and following your entrepreneurship dreams then you will want to understand what these traits are so that you can instill the same traits in yourself.

This will help ensure that you are able to achieve your dreams.

Successful Entrepreneurs:

- **Have passion and a lot of it**

- **Are tenacious**

- **Able to manage their fear of the unknown**

- **Have a grand vision**

- **Believe in themselves**

- **Are extremely flexible**

- **Are able to defy conventional wisdom**

- **Are willing to take risks in life**

If you have these traits, or if you can teach yourself how to develop these traits within yourself, then your likelihood of becoming a successful entrepreneur will increase. In addition to these personality traits, all successful entrepreneurs possess a certain amount of skills.

Skills That Will Help You to Become Sucessful in Business:

Focus - running your own business requires dealing with any number of factors on any given day. Successful business owners are able to pinpoint their focus onto accomplishing specific tasks and goals at specific times.

Resilience - it is a skill to be able to weather the various ups and downs of business without allowing them to destroy your focus. Truly successful entrepreneurs are able to continue traveling down the path of success even when the future looks bleak.

Management Skills - a successful company requires the right people and successful business owners need to know how to properly manage these people.

Long Term Vision - while it is easy to focus on what the company needs to do in the next several days or weeks to be successful, truly exceptional entrepreneurs (the ones who see real success in their business ventures) are able to plan years ahead of time.

Salesmanship - regardless of what type of company you are running, you need to be able to sell your vision to others in order to become successful. Entrepreneurs need to have great salesmanship skills whether they want to or not.

Self-reliance - this is one of the most important skills any entrepreneur can possess. It is vital for a business owner to trust that they can depend on themselves.

Self-reflection - the ability to pause, reflect and learn is a very valuable skill for the business owner. Entrepreneurs must be able to learn from their mistakes and reflect upon what they have learned in life.

Learning - the skill of earning knowledge is one that every successful business owner has. It is also a skill that they never stop developing.

To be successful in your entrepreneurial dreams you have to be able to learn from others. The best way to learn the skills of a successful business owner is to study the skills of successful entrepreneurs and then to grow those skills in yourself.

- Here you can find some of my TOP SECRET TIPS!!!

- Always choose something you are passionate about!

Without passion, and a lot of it, your business dreams will become lost in the day to day grind of running a business. Take a look at the top ten most successful entrepreneurs and you will see that their passion is the number one driving force behind their success. There is no way to escape this fact- you simply must be passionate in order to achieve your goals!

- Starting with a Dream!

The best way to start a business is to take what you are passionate about and find a way to turn that into a business. You need to start with a dream.

If you don't have passion for your work then you won't have the motivation and energy to keep pushing through obstacles, you won't be willing to take the necessary risks required to succeed and you won't be able to sell your dream to others.

Start with your dreams and grow your business from there.

The unfortunate reality is that once a business reaches the beginning of its third year its chances of surviving drops dramatically. Only about 44% of businesses live to see their fourth year. Without the passion you derive from living your dream you won't have what it takes to survive year after year. This means that you should start your business from the ground up using your dream as a foundation.

Whatever your dream in life may be, you need to find a way to turn that dream into a business. If the foundation of your business is based on something that you are truly passionate about, then it will be much easier to grow that dream into a hugely successful business.

- Starting Your Dream Business

Once you have determined that you have the necessary traits, skills and passion to become an entrepreneur, the next step will be to start up your dream business. You will need to commit tireless hours of work to get your business off the ground and getting it off the ground won't be enough. You must plow down all the obstacles in your path and never stop striving for greatness.

Getting Started

Getting started with your dream business may be the easiest part of the process or it may be the hardest. It really depends on your specific situation. Some would-be entrepreneurs are raring to get started, while others are bogged down with doubts and procrastination.

- Avoid coming up with excuses why you shouldn't start your own business.

Once you have made the important decision that yes you want to become an entrepreneur, skip the excuses and start the process.

Avoid the quicksand that is known as procrastination.

Putting off the process of starting your business for any reason can lead to getting stuck in the mud. Avoid the process of procrastination at all costs. What you do today will determine all your tommorws.

- Do whatever it takes to motivate yourself to get started.

Doubt, fear, worry and a lack of purpose can all end up preventing you from getting your dreams going. Focus on why you want to become an entrepreneur (your passion) and use that to motivate yourself into taking those first few steps. The first couple of steps are the most important ones.

- Develop core beliefs.

Now is the time to develop your business's core beliefs. This will help you to create the right kind of company, one that matches your passion and motivates you to always move forward. Your business's core beliefs will be a major building block of it, so make sure that these beliefs are worthy. They will also determine how you proceed to make decisions in the future and which direction the business takes your life. Making the Shift from Employee to Boss Running your own business takes leadership. For many new entrepreneurs it can be difficult to make the switch from employee to manager or boss. There are ways that you can prepare yourself for this transition. For people who have built-in leadership skills this transition may be easier, but anyone with the proper drive and motivation can develop leadership skills.

- Don't let the haters bring you down

There is one thing I have learned from my personal experiences. This is the simple saying "They hate you because they ain't you" and it resonated with me because it is simply true. People who are not as sucessful as you or who are pessimists will try to bring you down but you must block them out and take their words with a grain of salt and quite frankly as a compliment because people will talk about you when they envy you and the life you lead. Let them. This means you affected their lives. Don't let them affect yours. When someone reaches a certain point in their path to success people will do anything to invalidate what they have built. No one knows how much blood, sweat, and tears you have shed in order to reach your accomplishments but you. In certain cases, having tunnel vision is a good thing. When you are trying to build something, you must have your eye on the prize and never take it off until you get there.

9

WHAT DOES IT TAKE TO START AND RUN A BUSINESS?

Because you cannot get along with your boss and you have some cash in the bank to begin a business does not mean that it is the best thing to do for you. The truth is that owning a business is not for everyone. Not every person is made out to be an entrepreneur. Owning a business requires skill, aptitude and the right temperament. Before running head-over-heels into your first entrepreneurial venture you should take time to analyze who you are. When you invest your energy, time, and money in a business, you want a good return and therefore need to make sure that you have what it takes. While many entrepreneurs and small business owners make good money, there is no guarantee that you will do also.

Having a business means that you will have to confront your fears and handle a lot of trials. It is not without risks. To find out whether running your own business is for you, start small. If doable start part time. If you start part time you can test the waters and see if you really want to have your own business in the long run.

Owning a small business requires you to have the appropriate skills and personality. If you lack skills in a certain area, then you need to make adjustments and take some courses to beef up on your weak areas. There are many reasons for small business failure. However, if you possess most of the following skills and traits the chances of success will increase significantly:

Are You a Self-Starter?

If you are a self-starter you have a better chance of making it. Owning a business can be lonesome because you do not always have people that you can discuss problems with. You need to be able to take initiative to get things going and not rely on others to do it for you. This ability is especially important during the start-up phase.

Good People Skills are Important.

Even though you don't have to work with your boss or colleagues when you have your own business, you still are dealing with a lot of different people. That requires you to possess good people skills. People you probably deal with are business partners, customers, bankers, employees, contractors, accountants, lawyers, or other vendors in your industry. You need to be able to develop good rapport with a diverse group of people. Reputation is important in life in general, but especially when you are a business owner. Get along with people, and always aim for a win-win solution to business conflicts. That will go a long way in growing the business successfully.

Be a Decision Maker.

How are you when it comes to decision-making? Are you not afraid to make decisions? Your answer should be yes to that question as you can expect to be faced with situations that require you to make decisions quickly, efficiently, and independently. You need to be able to work through tough issues yourself and not be afraid to make decisions. Yes, you will make mistakes, but that is all part of learning.

Be Committed to Hard Work.

Running a business requires a lot of your time. You need to be able physically and emotionally 24 hours a day and 7 days a week. Not all the time, but when business requires such a commitment you must to be willing to step up to the plate and be there. If you are a family-oriented person, you will at times have to sacrifice family time. Research studies show that the first few years of the business are the most crucial as the business interferes with personal relationships. Even though your business will require total commitment at times, you must learn to balance personal and business. When things are slower make up for lost time with family and friends.

Set Goals and Objectives.

Do you set goals? If not, take some courses and learn how to plan and set goal and how to work toward them efficiently. You have heard the saying: "Failing to plan means planning to fail." A poor business plan or one with no plan at all, leads to business failure. Don't rush into things without a strong and well-designed plan.

As an entrepreneur you need to have perseverance and have a lot of patience. Do not fall for all the promotions that promise a quick get rich scheme. During these tough economic times you see more of these than ever, especially in internet marketing and MLM businesses. Do not fall for those slick sales pitches and do not rush too quickly into the next promising business opportunity. Success comes through hard work, commitment and good management. It also will take time.

There is no short cut to success no matter what others say.

10

THE BASICS OF SALES

MANAGEMENT FOR RESULTS

Whether you use a computerized or a manual system, the basics of selling are the same. There are tools and a system to follow which will bring you the desired results. This article is meant to give you the understanding of the sales management for results that take place after the sales activities are performed.

The sales activities are those that include the daily prospecting, calling and presenting of your products or service to get business. Basically, selling is a game of "using common sense, caring for your prospects and customers, knowing your product, calling and seeing a lot of people and asking them all to buy."

Whether you're just starting out selling or you have been selling for a while, you need to measure your results. If you can't measure it, you can't manage it. The system I use is all manual from selling activities to sales management but it can be applied to whatever type of system, even computerized - with minor adjustment.

Here are the tools to manage and measure the results of your sales activities:

Sales Management Tool #1 - The Daily Activity Sheets

Sales Management Tool #2 - The Weekly Activity Reports

Sales Management Tool #3 - The Monthly summary

Sales Management Tool #4 - The Performance Graph

These sheets which you title as above and insert into a binder, are where you keep track of your daily, weekly, monthly performance. You can also use sales software rather then do it the old fashion way. How many cold calls, sales calls, sales presentations and sales per day, per week per month. This will give you all the ratios you need to perform and out-perform your activities. This is where you will find out how many cold calls it takes to get a sales call, to get a sales presentation, to close a sale. Then every time you want to improve, you simply up these numbers where you see appropriate.

The daily activities sheets turn into the weekly reports and the weekly reports turn into the monthly summaries. Then the monthly figures turn into the graph (Tool #4) that begins to take shape. When you do your 20-30 hourly calls at the beginning, and then the increasing follow-up and service calls after 4 weeks, the figures will tell you the specifics about the product you sell - the ratio of phone calls to appointments and appointments to sales that you figure out in your Tools #1, 2, 3.

With this information, you will now be on your way to become an expert - a professional. You will get the benchmarks needed to make the results go anywhere you want. If your number of calls were too low last week or last month, you can step it up from these figures. If you want to increase any categories of your Sales Activities, i.e. Cold Calls, Appointments, Presentations, Closings, etc., you can make it happen from here. When you have these figures, you can manage your efforts and have control over your own productivity and results.

However, to know your product is not enough in these tough economic times. You must know your industry, your competition, your buyer, yourself. And you must believe in your product or service. To see a lot of people is important, because sales is a numbers game. But, qualifying the door you knock on and knowing when to knock requires some preparation and research about your prospect and his/her needs.

Asking all to buy is a must, but without being intrusive or overbearing, and only when the customer is ready. I always say that you cannot sell until someone buys. And someone will buy only when they discover that they can trust you, you know the solution to their need and you can deliver that solution to their expectation. That's when they're ready.

Using common sense is the key in everything we do. One must consider and respect the customer's pride, and not offend, insult or talk more than necessary.

11

RULES TO BUILD A WILDLY SUCCESSFUL BUSINESS

But wait, because there's one more thing. In fact, 10 more.

Goldman and Nalebuff share 10 must-follow rules on how to start and build an equally impressive empire.

1. "Build something you believe in -- because that's the first step to building a great brand."

Just like Goldman and Nalebuff, I learned a powerful lesson in tenacious passion from years of entrepreneurship. When you're all alone, sitting in a dark room wondering why your business is failing, there is only one true thing to power you forward -- you believe in your purpose.

2. "Don't aim for 10% improvement. Make it radically better and different."

Yes -- in today's society we collectively create amazing products, services and companies through entrepreneurship. World changing at times and Honest Tea was radically different when first introduced. But, if you look around, we also live in the land of 'me-too' businesses. Don't fall for it. Dig deep and decide right now to build something radically different and radically better.

3. **"Prepare to be copied. Don't start unless you'll survive imitation."**

If your idea is truly radical and takes off, you can count the minutes before the copy-cats arrive. How will you survive competition from the big 800-pound gorillas on the block? Or even from the upstart little guys? Your key is a system of 'continuous innovation'. Although you could also take the road of Honest Tea -- make friends with one of the gorillas and let them buy you out. (Coca-Cola Company acquired Honest Tea in 2011.)

4. **"Build up reserves of money and energy for bad luck and mistakes."**

Great advice -- but sometimes extremely difficult to do. What startup or growth company has reserves of cash sitting around? But Goldman and Nalebuff make a good point -- run as lean as you possibly can and do not waste money or energy. You will endure mistakes and bad luck along the way, so having a good war chest full of capital and energy can help handle it.

5. "Never, ever give up control -- until you sell."

Some high-impact entrepreneurs will readily give up control in exchange for the lure of high-growth through venture capital -- but I am not one of them. Relinquish control and you risk losing the culture and vision of the company you set out to build. Even though Honest Tea raised investment capital from the beginning, the co-founders always remained in the driver's seat. (And yes -- Goldman can still drive his vision as CEO of Honest Tea, but his boss at Coca-Cola can say 'no' at anytime. Thus, true control is forever gone.)

6. "Don't compromise on the big things -- compromise on everything else."

Vision. Purpose. Core values. Write these things in stone and never budge. But flexibility in the value propositions, products and services you build to execute your purpose is vastly important. Many entrepreneurs I see fail to 'bend to the market' by adapting to what their customer's are telling them.

7. "Figure out how to achieve your goals on a tiny budget -- then cut that number in half."

Yes -- you've heard it said before -- it will cost twice as much, and take twice as long as you think. My recommendation is you apply the principles of lean to your business from day one. No fancy offices. No fancy full color brochures. Your goal is to stay alive until you can nail your secret formula for success. Blowing the budget will insure nothing but a quick death.

8. "It's a marathon, not a sprint."

Is it ever. Building a business is neither for the faint of heart or the speed demon. Climbing Mt. Everest is not done in 3 easy steps: 1.) decide you want to do it, 2.) fly to Nepal with zero preparation, 3.) sprint straight up the mountain in 12 easy minutes. Build systems for the long-haul and focus on small-connected steps. (It takes 26,364 steps of 7" each to climb Mt. Everest, and that's starting from half way up at Basecamp.)

9. "Take care of your family, personal and spiritual health -- if you aren't laughing or smiling on a regular basis, recalibrate."

Imagine the path to a wildly successful business: founder working at a feverish pitch for 18 hours each day, for at least 5 years straight.

True? No, it's not. Goldman flat-out said two reasons he made it through the rough years: first -- he believed in his purpose, second -- his drive for personal balance. The notion we need to kill our family relationships, personal health or level of sanity to build our own business is sadly misaligned. Take it from me -- don't go there.

10. "Build the enterprise and the brand as if you'll own them forever."

Will you sell your business someday? Maybe. Should that be the sole reason you are building it? Probably not. When you start and build a business based on passion and purpose, with a burning desire to solve the pain of your customer through the deliverance of monetizable value, you build a far more valuable enterprise. Those in it for the short-term quick buck rarely succeed. Your company should be an extentsion of yourself and treated like a baby. You must give it much attention and watch it grow exponentially.

Plaster these 10 rules from Goldman and Nalebuff to your mirror, live by them everyday of your life as an entrepreneur and you might end up as successful as they. Honest.

12

CLIMBING THE LADDER TO SUCCESS

To be a most successful entrepreneur you will need to have above all else self-confidence and an unshakable belief in your abilities. You have to be dedicated, willing to work long and hard, take disappointments in your stride, shake off failure and move on, learn from your mistakes and not lose sight of your end goal, which means staying potent.

As Gordon Ramsey, world renowned chef and Michelin star winner puts it, to become the most successful entrepreneur, "the secret is to make sure the business is running to perfection with or without me". You will find that this holds true in the case of each and every successful entrepreneur. People start out with nothing more than dreams or visions and a lot of self confidence. They have the grit and determination to turn those dreams and visions into reality - real, live businesses that help them attain most successful entrepreneur status.

There are many lessons to be learned from the success stories of prosperous entrepreneurs, who started from scratch with nothing more than a desire to become the most successful entrepreneur.

Bill Gates needs no introduction; he began programming at the age of 13 but he had a dream he later turned into Microsoft Corporation. This dream turned reality, kept this most successful entrepreneur on the top of the pile as richest man in the world for a long time.

Ben & Jerry, think yummy ice cream! Ben Cohen and Jerry Greenfield began their career working in a gas station! Much toil, struggle and failure marked their path to success. Today they can each be considered among the most successful entrepreneurs, right up there with all the other success stories.

Oprah Winfrey's name is synonymous with entertainment. This mega personality has ascended heights beyond description - she had a dream and she worked very hard on it. Today she is truly worthy of most successful entrepreneur status.

There are many men and women who have had the passion and the drive to turn visions to reality. What drove them? One of the main elements you will find through research is time management. If you do not have this skill the results you will attain will only be mediocre at the best.

To become the most successful entrepreneur, you need to develop your time management skills to such a high degree of perfection that not a minute spent is wasted. You have to expect, anticipate and work towards making every minute of every day produce results. No! It is not recommended that you work to the exclusion of all else; however producing results in all areas of your life will bring a sense of cohesiveness and harmony.

Needless to say, to become the most successful entrepreneur requires a dream to start of with. Then you take all of your dedication, will power, commitment and motivation and pour it into building a business; add inspiration and innovation and you will have a recipe for success. What you do today will determine all your tommorows.

PART 2

Becoming a Leader

"If your actions inspire others to dream more, learn more, do more and become more, you are a leader." John Quincy Adams

Leadership is a hot topic. You see it everywhere - books on leadership, leadership seminars, management leadership training, and non-profit and business leadership courses abound. It's a hot topic because it's important, and because traditional leadership qualities and strategies are being challenged by new research that is showing that people respond to leadership differently than they used to. Expectations have changed, and the thinking around what makes a good leader has changed as well. This section starts with Growing the Leader in You which will help put you on track toward becoming a leader people will want to follow. Sometimes strong leaders simply stray from their original focus or path due to the constant daily demands of owning a small business. Achieving Clarity offers guidance to help you re-define your vision as the leader of your company and to create a clearer vision for the future of your small business. In addition, you'll find valuable leadership strategies that include developing an ethical workplace, assessing your business effectiveness, and the art of delegation. Whatever the time of the year, it's always worth making a few new resolutions. Finally, take some time to think about what you might need to do in order to get ready to sell your business or pass it on to the next generation. As a small business owner, you are a leader. Whether you're leading your business all on your own, or have a team that looks up to you for leadership, these chapters will help you to think about things differently, and inspire and equip you to grow your leadership skills in the coming years.

14

Transitioning from Managing to Leading

The trend towards a distinction between managing vs management is progressing rapidly in today's business culture, and those who are being led rather than managed are showing signs of greater productivity, increased job satisfaction and a higher potential than ever before. The paradigm shift that must take place in this transition from managing to leading can be quite substantial, depending on both your management style and your employment history. If you're an authoritative type who functions best when there are lots of rules and standards, and everyone is being managed to adhere to those standards, you may have more difficulty making the shift than someone who is by nature an open team player who enjoys participation with others more than achieving standards. Whatever your natural style, the trend toward leadership is growing, and the result of teams operating in this way is encouraging. Let's have a look at the difference between a manager and a leader. MANAGERS Managers manage because they are working in a hierarchy. By definition, a manager has a higher position than those who work for him/her, and who over another group of people, make decisions about how those people will work and evaluate their performance. It is a formal authority within a hierarchical structure. The subordinates do what they are told to do and their salary is often the primary motivator for their performance. Managers are typically also subordinates to someone else, and are paid to get a job done using their subordinate workforce. This translates into productivity being of primary importance to the manager, since the performance of the workforce reflects on their management performance. According to recent research, managers tend to be people who have come from stable backgrounds and lead relatively comfortable lives. They tend not to be risk takers. In a hierarchical workforce, it is important that the team looks upon the manager as more knowledgeable and less prone to making mistakes than they are. LEADERS Leaders, by contrast, do not have subordinates. Even if they are working in hierarchical organizations, they choose to give up their formal authority and invite people to follow. Leaders tend to have a more charismatic style and understand that telling people what to do does not necessarily inspire them to follow you. They tend to be more people-focused than task-focused and are always interested in seeing growth and development in those they are leading. This does not mean a leader cannot be task-focused - in fact, many are, but they know how to encourage loyalty and motivate others to work toward common goals and visions. Leaders appear to be much more likely to take risks. They are comfortable with making changes when problems come along, and are not afraid of conflict and confrontation for the betterment of the team. Leaders willingly admit their mistakes, and use them as learning tools for the team. The trend of making a transition from management to leadership is occurring because studies show people are less motivated by money and highly motivated by job satisfaction, the feeling of making a difference and doing meaningful work that is valued by others. People in general prefer to be led rather than managed. Traditional management still works and functions in our culture, however a leadership style of management produces greater results. Leadership expert and author

Jim Clemmer says, "Leadership is a verb, not a noun. It is action, not a position. It is what we do, not the role we are in." If you have the freedom in your business to make the behavioral and visionary transition from managing your employees to leading them, it may be well worth the effort to see the difference it could make. Even if you are working within a company structure, you can adopt a leadership philosophy within your management style. How can you make this transition with those you manage? Here are some suggestions:

1) **Work alongside them rather than above them**

Let them know you are more interested in working with them than in just managing them.

2) **Invite the input of those you work with.**

This does not mean you are bound to accept every piece of advice or suggestion given to you, but if you truly consider every person's input and value their willingness to give it to you, you will inspire them.

3) **Remove hierarchical language from your workplace**.

Language is a powerful thing, and it can influence the way people view themselves and how others view you. Begin introducing co-workers as people you work with, rather than people who work for you.

4) **Provide an atmosphere conducive to teamwork.**

Create opportunities for staff to contribute their ideas and thoughts about what's happening in the business.

5) **Provide teamwork training for strengthening your team.**

Acknowledge the successes of individuals when they reach their goals or deliver exceptional performance.

6) **Share the load.**

When one person is struggling beneath a heavy workload, pass it on - this fosters a shared sense of purpose and teamwork within the company.

7) **Be vulnerable with your team.**

Let them know where you struggle, and where your weaknesses are. They will respect you for your authenticity and be more motivated to put their shoulders to the wheel and help out when you need it.

The transition from managing to leading can produce great results. Try making a few changes to see how your team responds. If you get the results that are typical with this kind of transition, you will find your team working harder, faster and better than ever before.

15

ETHICAL BUSINESS AND BUSINESS PLACE ETHICS

Ethical business and workplace ethics are popular topics these days. More and more organizations are enlisting business to join them under the umbrella of ethical businesses practices, products and services. Ethics consultants are being hired to help companies see how they can establish ethical workplaces. Just because it's hot, doesn't mean you should drop everything and hire a consultant. However, here's some food for thought. For some business owners, the desire to establish ethical business practices may come from having experienced unethical treatment somewhere else. They want everyone connected with their business to know that they will be treated ethically. For others, it's simply an affirmation of what they're already doing. They run values-based ethical businesses, but having documentation that outlines their ethical policies simply formalizes the fact that they're doing it. If you've never thought about it before, here are a few reasons to consider building an ethical workplace.

ETHICAL BUSINESS PRACTICES IMPROVE SOCIETY

Fair wages, workplace safety, discrimination, sexism, child labor – all are issues that have been addressed as a result of business ethics. A willingness over the years by employees to raise, and employers to address, unfair work practices has resulted in much higher employment standards than existed several decades ago.

ETHICS PROGRAMS CULTIVATE STRONG TEAMS AND INCREASE PRODUCTIVITY

An ethical business program is built on the moral and ethical values of its leaders. Your business ethics will reflect your values and what's important to you. If you're a savvy business owner, you hire people who believe in and support those values; people who are willing to reflect the behaviors and standards of those ethical values. In an ethical workplace, everyone knows where they stand, as well as the resulting consequences if they fall outside of the ethical guidelines set for the business. A common purpose, shared vision and clear expectations all contribute to a strong team, and a desire on behalf of team members to do well for the company, resulting in greater productivity.

ETHICS PROGRAMS PROTECT EVERYONE

If workplace ethics are clearly laid out in company policy, and if employees have agreed to those policies, legal action against employers becomes more difficult. On the other hand, ethics also protect employees from shady business practices of their employers. Not too many business owners will agree to write down their unethical practices in a document. If a company supports ethical business practices, everyone wins. Ethical Business Practices Provide a Moral Compass for the Company Because ethics are values-based, they will not move with the winds of change. They won't change as new technology arises, they won't change when staff or management come and go, and they won't change when others in the industry do. They are like a beacon that defines who you are as a business, and how you function, no matter what else is going on around you. This sets a strong foundation for your business and allows you to do business in your industry with integrity and stability.

ETHICS PROGRAMS HELP YOU MANAGE YOUR BUSINESS

In every area of your business – policy, production, service, administration, planning – your ethics guide you. They are the foundation of everything that happens. Spelling out your workplace ethics means that those principles guide your decisions in every area. It means your managers know what decision you'd make in any given circumstance, and follow suit. It means employees know how you want them to behave. It means everyone knows and agrees with how you want to run your business.

AN ETHICAL BUSINESS PROJECTS A STRONG PUBLIC IMAGE

You will become known by your practices. If people know you honor your contracts, put out only the highest quality products, value them as customers, and do what you can to make things right when they go wrong, they will make a decision about whether to do business with you. Ethical business practices are valued by the public, and can only improve your business success. An ethical organization demonstrates the following principles:

1. They value diversity

2. They are zealously committed to fairness

3. They focus on individual rather than collective responsibility

4. They don't do anything that isn't tied to their overall purpose

5. They have a clear vision

16

7 TRAITS OF SUCCESSFUL LEADING ENTREPRENEURS

All of us have skills, talents and experience that position us in the marketplace to do certain jobs really well. Some of these things are learned in a formal way, some are learned through experience, and some are innate– they're just the way we're made. In the same way that you can see the qualities that would make someone a good counselor (listening skills, empathy, discernment, patience), or a great carpenter (attention to detail, accuracy, skilled hands, pride in their work), you can also determine the traits that make a successful entrepreneur. Some of these traits can be learned, but many are hard-wired. Entrepreneurs are a special breed. They fearlessly take risks, plunge forward without always having all the information, are willing to suffer the consequences of making mistakes, and for the most part

– can't imagine being employees! Here are seven traits that you'll see in most leading entrepreneurs. Just like the counselor and the carpenter, these are the things that make entrepreneurs successful in the crazy, ever changing, competitive world of business.

Bounce-Back Buoyancy

All companies go through highs and lows in terms of sales cycles, productivity, staffing, cash flow and many other aspects of business. How you weather those highs and especially the employment lows will affect the overall success. What do you do when your cash flow starts to dip into negative territory? Or when you aren't reaching your sales targets? And what about those times when you're struggling to keep enough staff to run the business? What is your attitude when you make mistakes – botch a huge order, upset an important customer, or miss a critical deadline? Your ability to "bounce back" in all these areas is extremely important. Do you have systems in place for when the "low times" occur so that you can keep running effectively? Have you thought through how you'll deal with mistakes if and when they happen? Entrepreneurs have a plan before the tough times arrive to ensure they'll be able to weather those storms and bounce back more quickly.

Necessary Nurture

Although much has been written about the importance of staff development and employee morale for a successful company, this point cannot be overstated. Are you providing an open environment where people feel free to voice their opinions, ideas, complaints, and suggestions? Are you approachable – does your staff feel it's safe to come to you with their concerns? Do you provide opportunities for continued learning and skill building? When your staff is healthy and happy, your customers will benefit, and ultimately your company will see growth and success. Successful entrepreneurs take the time to nurture the people who give them one-third of their lives every day. This is a critical component of success.

Going with Your Gut

Intuition is one of those funny things that everyone has, but not everyone trusts. Intuition is not so much the power of knowing what's going to happen, but the power of observing what is happening. Entrepreneurs observe what's going on around them, and the more they do, the stronger (and more accurate) their intuition becomes. For example, if you notice a change in the dynamic of how your staff interacts on a daily basis (whispering in small groups, normally social people working behind closed doors, underlying tension at staff meetings), your intuition kicks in and tells you something is wrong and you need to pay attention. Entrepreneurs have honed their powers of observation with staff, customers, competitors, and within their industries, resulting in an ability to anticipate and troubleshoot problems before they get out of hand.

Capacity for Creativity

Best-selling business author George Lois said, "Creativity can solve almost any problem. The creative act, the defeat of habit by originality, overcomes everything." This could not be truer for business owners. Creativity is seeing something that doesn't already exist. It's looking beyond the obvious "same-old" solutions even if those solutions have been effective in the past. It's finding new ways to sell, new ways to exceed customer expectations, new ways to motivate and encourage employees, new ways to solve old problems, and new ways to plan for your future. Brainstorming, mind-mapping, focus groups, and sometimes simple, casual get-togethers with friends and coworkers can spawn creative ideas that will impact business in a big way. Maintaining an atmosphere that says "no idea is a bad idea", and giving people the freedom to drop things into the hopper will shake things up now and again. Entrepreneurs depend on a constant infusion of creativity to navigate the changing business climates they face

Passionate Productivity

People often start businesses because they have a passion to do or create something that they want to share or provide to others. After a few years, the demand of simply running the business can begin to take over any passion that may still be lingering, and rather than a passionate offering of a product or service, it becomes a daily grind. Successful entrepreneurs find a way to continuously reclaim that passion. They find new ways to do old things. They make changes that fuel them and move their businesses forward. They welcome ideas. They constantly look at their business from different angles with a view to making it better. Passion is contagious, and successful entrepreneurs have it in spades.

Living Leadership

Successful entrepreneurs are the leaders of their businesses. The impact of that statement is enormous, and those who take it seriously have successful companies. Everyone is watching the leader – staff, customers, competitors – and how the business is run is being noticed by everyone they come in contact with. Someone once said that integrity is defined by what you do when you think no one is watching. Entrepreneurs take advantage of the awesome responsibility of leading their company. They recognize people are always watching, and live out their values and principles in everything they do. They embrace their personality, leadership style, strengths and weaknesses, experience, and passion, and live them out on a daily basis. Living leadership is a noticeable trait in successful business owners

Boldness in Balance

Balancing home and work successfully is absolutely a critical skill for successful entrepreneurs. It takes boldness to set boundaries, to be willing to make tough choices and to prioritize in a way that provides balance in all areas of life. If business is controlling your life, you may feel successful in the short term, but the toll on your family and your life will be great. The long-term consequences won't be worth it. Entrepreneurs understand their personal lives deserve attention as much as their businesses. Maintaining strong relationships, volunteering to serve others, having hobbies and interests beyond work – all of these create balance, and a balanced person is a much more effective business owner. How many of these leadership entrepreneurial traits do you exhibit? They may be things you have inside of you, but somehow, you've let them take a back seat. Are there goals you could set to bring them out and make them a part of how you run your business and ultimately lead you to greater success?

PART 3

HOW TO SELL ANYTHING, ANYWHERE and DEVELOP A BRAND IMAGE

For first-time and experienced entrepreneurs, this section is created as a guide that reviews the process of planning and executing a startup's Go to Market Strategy (GTM) by using examples, offering insight. At the end of every section there is a segment that offers suggestions for appropriate metrics that can be used to measure the success of each aspect of your strategy. You will learn how to sucesfully execute a campaign to develop a brand for you new company. Not all the suggested metrics provided in this section will be appropriate for your specific business and it is encouraged for you to create several of your own metrics that are not provided. It is my hope that this material comes in handy and helps you jumpstart your company and upscale the same.

17

(STEP ONE)

UNDERSTANDING THE GO TO MARKET STRATEGY

"How you sell stuff" is the simplest way to explain a Go to Market Strategy. When you are completing a GTM Strategy, these four questions are very important questions you have to keep in mind.

1) What are you selling?

2) Who are you selling it to?

3) How will you reach your target market?

4) Where will you promote your product?

Start with the end in mind. As much as possible, initially try to consider how you will succeed and build your company around that vision from day #1. Here's an example of that methodology:

Every GTM strategy will be different. No one company is going to sell its products and services the same way. Consider past sales and revenue trends. If you've already been in business prior to creating your GTM strategy, then make sure you review your past marketing and selling tactics and results. You can also gain insight from the strategies and tactics established competitors in your industry (or similar industries) use to reach their customers.

Segmenting: Who Is Your Target Customer?

A "target market" or "target customer" is a group of potential customers who you intend to be the recipients of your marketing efforts. Often target customers will be identified as a group of people or organizations that have similar needs or pain points that your product/service looks to address Identifying.

Identify Your Target Market:

Identifying your target market will likely require a deep understanding of your customer and their needs. This knowledge can be obtained through: Collecting data from market research that's already been collected by reports and studies by government agencies, trade associations or other businesses. This is referred to as secondary market research. You do this by collecting data through your own primary market research efforts using surveys and speaking directly to customers. This is often called "Customer Discovery". Continue to ask yourself "what are the common needs or pain points of the people or organizations that make up my target market?". Ensure the commonalities are easily distinguishable.

Keep it Focused! Expand on Success, Don't Contract on Failure

Early-stage companies are often ambitious and make the mistake of considering "Everybody is our customer" or "anyone with a smartphone is our customer"] Startups are strapped for money, time, and other resources. It requires a lot of resources for a company to try to attract "everybody" as their customer. Young companies should dominate a smaller market then expand to a larger market as opposed to initially failing to reach a larger market and having to then refocus on a smaller segment. A Minimum Viable Segment (MVS) is a market that is focused enough that your product/service can dominate by meeting the common needs of the customers in the segment. MVS methodology allows a you to quickly and cheaply validate potential markets o If initially the assumed target customer isn't a good fit, the company will have ideally saved enough marketing resources to try a different segment.

DEVELOPING CUSTOMER PERSONAS

Buyer personas (or marketing personas) are fictional, generalized representations of the exact customers that you are trying to attract. By creating fake characters like "Attorney Anthony" or "Manager Molly" you can make it easier to see your customers as real people.

For example, let's say your ideal customer is someone you name "Manager Molly" Just a few of the many characteristics that you may assign to her may be:

- She is in her 30s with a college degree
- She hasn't been in a management role for more than 2 years
- She is ambitious and wants the attention of senior management

Imagining Manager Molly as a real person who has all those attributes can help you consider her deepest needs and how to effectively market to her. If you have multiple audiences, initially go for the one with the deepest need. Sometimes a business will have two (or more) very different types of potential customer markets and will need to decide which group to target first.

For example, Google has 2 customers—

1) The everyday person who uses the search engine

2) The companies who pay for Google AdWords advertisement

It's advised that you thoroughly examine each market, then initially target the one you determine has the greatest need/pain points that your solution solves.

Measure Everything! Suggestions for what to measure

Estimate the size of each segmented market. If overtime you go after multiple target markets, measure how each market compares in regard to the sales revenue customer acquisition costs, length of sales cycle, buying habits, market penetration rate, etc.?

18

(STEP TWO)

VALUE PROPOSITION:

WHAT DO YOU OFFER AND

HOW IS IT DIFFERENT?

POSITIONING:

Market positioning is the effort of attempting to influence your customer's perception of your brand or product/service relative to their feelings toward your competitors' brands or product/services. Effective positioning will allow your brand or product/service to occupy a clear, unique, and advantageous position in the customer's mind. Imagine you sold smart watches. See below for an illustration of how your smartwatch's features of waterproofness and data storage could set your product apart from the competition in a customer's mind.

DETERMINING YOUR VALUE PROPOSITION

A Value Proposition requires an understanding of Your target customer, Common needs or pain points your target possess that sets them apart, the category of products/services you compete in, the distinct value(s) your solution offers your target customers and how your product/service provides the stated distinct values.

ARTICULATING YOUR VALUE PROPOSITION

To position your product/service, it is important to be able to clearly articulate your value proposition within your organization and within your messaging to your customers. One common structure for a value proposition statement is: "For target who are segment, [insert name of brand/product/service] is a category that provides distinct value(s) by/through/because solution"

WHO IS YOUR TARGET CUSTOMER?

Let's say your poduct is a smart watch and let's say your target audience are "professionals". To clarify, this means that you are not targeting entire organizations, amateurs, or hobbyists. What common attribute(s) do your target customers possess that segments them apart from others? A fully waterproof smart watch with high data storage might be most useful for people whose professions require them to work underwater while collecting significant amount of data. How successful they are at their job is greatly affected by the functionality of the tools they use. For example, consider a deep-sea marine biologist as someone who may find this product useful. What category of products/services do you compete in? The category would likely be "smart watches". People in your target market are likely, in general, familiar with what a smart watch is. If you referred to your product as something that is less familiar or vaguer, like a "portable data storage device", then your target might have difficulty understanding what you sell.

WHAT ARE THE DISTINCT VALUE(S) YOU OFFER YOUR TARGET CUSTOMERS?

The smart watch provides the value of complete underwater protection for mass amounts of data. How do you provide the distinct values? Concisely explain your solution. The smart watch provides the value of complete underwater protection for mass amounts of data through "revolutionary pressure control and compact data storage technology" Complete Value Proposition Statement: "For professionals who perform underwater data collection, the Deep-Sea Turbo 5000 is a smart watch that provides complete underwater protection for mass amounts of data through revolutionary pressure control and compact data storage technology"

PAY CLOSE ATTENTION TO WHAT YOUR COMPETITION IS DOING

In order to effectively position your solution, it is important to regularly and thoroughly monitor your competition and their offerings. Your positioning may change as new products or competitors enter your market.

MEASURE EVERYTHING!

Discover what your customers value most. Don't just guess what they value, ask them. Then attempt to identify metrics that allow you to measure the ability of your solution to deliver those values versus that of your competitors' solutions. For example, if your customers cared about speed, then measure and compare the speed of your product and your competitors' products. If you experiment with multiple value propositions, identify metrics that will help you determine which one was most effective. (Ex: sales, views, shares, etc.).

19

(STEP THREE)

BRANDING:

HOW DO YOU WANT TO BE PERCEIVED?

WHAT DEFINES A BRAND?

Vision – What about the world is changing that makes your company necessary? Where do you see your business and brand being in 5 years? 10? 20+ years?

Promise – What do you promise to customers at the most fundamental level? Note the example promises are fundamental (not necessarily specific)

Attributes – What makes you different, better, and unique? Emotion – From a customer's perspective, what does it feel like to engage with you?

THE EVOLUTION OF A BRAND:

ACCEPT THAT YOU'LL LOSE CONTROL

In the very beginning of the life of a startup the brand embodies the founders. As the company grows, the perceived brand will be represented by the employees, the company culture, and the execution of business operations. Before a startup introduces its product/service into the market, the story of the brand will be told by the company. At this point, founders have a lot of control over the brand. Once the product/service is available, the market will begin to tell your brand's story. At this point, your customers will develop and share their own perceptions of your brand.

DON'T INITIALLY OVER-PROMISE

For example: imagine that before you launched, you initially conveyed that you were a luxury brand. If customers begin to use your product and they perceive it as far less than luxury, you may find that you over-promised. Startups often make the mistake of initially over-promising what their brand offers. Brand image can suffer when you over-promise and under-deliver. Consider the promises that you can over-deliver on and initially convey those. Be realistic. Don't over-promise but also don't be so cautious that you undersell. Initially, you can convey what your solution offers at the most fundamental level. Then let satisfied customers sell others on the additional benefits they recognize that your product/service can deliver. A Brand Has To Be Consistent. Just like in personal relationships, individuals want to be able to depend on your brand to be consistent in the products/services it delivers and how it markets. You want to consistently deliver in meeting your customer's expectations.

MEASURE EVERYTHING!

Identify metrics for your marketing efforts and products/services that can be measured in order to determine if you are staying true to your brand. For example, a restaurant may regularly measure the shape and weight of its cheeseburgers to ensure that those measurements remain consistent. Continually poll and listen to your customers to ensure your brand has remain consistent and that it is fulfilling all its promises.

Branding is similarly as vital for private companies as it is for enormous names. Without a doubt, numerous corporate brands endeavour to look more like little firms keeping in mind the end goal to engage customers that want to help autonomous brands.

For some entrepreneurs, branding is basic to their business, yet a shockingly high number of them don't generally know why.

They perceive the connection between fruitful organizations and solid branding and seek to construct a brand that copies comparable accomplishment for themselves. Furthermore, they comprehend that branding isn't only a logo or how their business is seen remotely. In any case, excessively few understand that effective brands have this branding at the core of the business. To such an extent that from multiple points of view you could relatively substitute the word brand for business.

The advantages that a deliberately characterized brand can bring are the same as when individuals experience passionate feelings for each other. At the point when clients interface emotively - in light of the fact that they share similar esteems and convictions of a brand - it prompts higher deals and better brand separation. It likewise prompts devotion, backing and can even secure your cost in times when contenders depend on limited time rebates to drive deals. It can likewise give you the perfect stage from which to broaden your offering or range.

Branding is a method for characterizing your business to yourself, your group and your outside gatherings of people. It could be known as the business' "character", yet just on the understanding that it encapsulates the center of what the business is and it esteems, not exactly what it looks and seems like. Clients of a wide range of organizations are so insightful today that they can see through most endeavors by organizations to gleam, turn or appeal their approach to deals.

The brand picture is everything in the present vicious business condition and day in and day out news and data cycle. Despite your industry, you require a stone strong brand to emerge from contenders and catch clients' consideration.

Building a Foundation for a Strong Brand Image

The ideal approach to assemble and support a powerful brand picture is through a multidisciplinary approach that joins claimed, earned and paid media in a planned, computerized biological community developed of PR, social, seek and different components.

There are a few prerequisites that you'll have to address as you build up your brand picture:

Distinguish Your Key Audiences: The initial step is to recognize your intended interest groups. Your intended interest groups will comprise of a blend of outside and inner gatherings, including clients, accomplices, industry investigators, and workers. It's imperative to be particular when characterizing your crowds. You require lucidity about the gatherings you are focusing to create a viable promoting technique that will talk straightforwardly to their one of a kind needs and concerns.

Decide Critical Business Goals: You need to know where you are going before you can arrive. Building a brand picture without knowing your here and now and long-haul business objectives is ineffectual and a misuse of profitable assets.

Characterize Your Brand Persona: Once you have decided your key gatherings of people and basic business objectives, you can begin to work out your brand persona. Your persona should engage clients and well-spoken your most vital differentiators and item benefits. Since your brand persona characterizes your picture, it's vital to keep it straightforward and pertinent.

Create Key Messaging: After you've characterized your brand persona and picture, archive your key messages and adjust them to your gatherings of people. Your key messages will be the most vital takeaways you need your group of onlookers to leave within the wake of collaborating with your brand. They should join the one of a kind part of your business and esteem added to clients, with a sprinkle of your brand identity.

Subsequent stages of Solidifying Your Brand Image: After you have penetrated down and established the framework for your brand picture, you can increase your advancement exercises to manufacture a devoted client following and create deals. The three segments that are important to advance your brand on a wide scale include:

Advertising: Advertising disperses your key messages and news in online web journals, social media platforms, exchange productions, and news outlets. By situating your organization as an idea pioneer and master source on breaking news and patterns, PR can enhance your brand picture and bring issues to light.

Content: Content is the fuel that drives coordinated PR and computerized showcasing exercises. To hoist your brand profile, you'll have to convey a constant flow of white papers, contributed articles, blog entries and other rich substance resources for target gathering of people sections.

Social: Social media is a profitable device for sharing data pertinent to your industry and communicating with clients and influencers in your field. A hearty web-based social networking nearness can fundamentally build site movement and upgrade your picture with both new and existing clients.

Search: Search Engine Optimization (SEO) is a strategy that enhances your organization's positioning on well-known web crawlers like Google. To have an effect on key gatherings of people, you'll have to rank well for particular catchphrases and key expressions, expanding the measure of activity to your organization site and other computerized resources.

Here are tips on how to successfully implement branding for your business.

1. **Begin by characterizing your brand**

Survey the item or administration your business offers, pinpoint the space in the market it involves and inquires about the emotive and judicious needs and worries of your clients. Your brand character ought to advance your business, associated with your client base and separate you in the market.

2. When assembling your brand, consider it a man

Each one of us is a person whose character is comprised of convictions, qualities, and purposes that characterize our identity and who we associate with. Our identity decides how we carry on in various circumstances, how we dress and what we say. Obviously, for individuals it's instinctive and it's uncommon that you considerably consider what your own character is, yet when you're fabricating a brand have that understanding.

3. Consider what is driving your business

What does it put stock in, what is its motivation and who are its brand saints? These things can help build up your emotive brand situating and educate the personality and character of brand correspondences.

4. Intend to fabricate long haul associations with your clients

Try not to spruce up your offering and bring desires that outcome up in broken guarantees, make trust with genuine branding - be clear who your organization is and be consistent with the qualities that drive it consistently.

5. Address your clients with a steady manner of speaking

It will help fortify the business' character and elucidate its offering so clients know precisely what's in store for the item or administration.

6. **Try not to rehash a similar message similarly again and again**

On the other hand, expect to influence your key messages to cooperate to manufacture a lucid character.

7. **Try not to attempt to mirror the look of chains or enormous brands.**

Attempt and cut out your own particular personality. There is a major customer incline towards free foundations, and a few chains are in certainty attempting to impersonate an autonomous feel to catch some of that market. Genuinely free administrators can use their status to draw in clients who are searching for something more unique and bona fide, that lines up with how to feel about themselves.

8. **Be imaginative, striking and brave** - remain for something you trust in

Huge brands are burdened by extensive layers of organization, keeping them from being adaptable and responding to the consistently changing requirements of their clients. Those layers of leaders can make it difficult for them to set out with their branding.

9. **Continuously think about your branding when speaking with clients**

Try not to lose your pride or weaken your brand situating with aimless marking down. Have a go at offering all the more, as opposed to slicing costs. Advancements are a chance to fortify your brand mission.

10. **The old method for stamping your logo on everything won't cut it**

The fate of branding is liquid and connecting with - regarding your clients' insight by not surrendering everything without end front. Create some interest and enable them to uncover more about your brand for themselves. This is the best approach to cultivate representatives who delight in telling other individuals what they have found.

Characterizing Your Brand

Defining your brand is a journey of business self-discovery. It can be difficult, time-consuming and uncomfortable. It requires, at the very least, that you answer the questions below

What is your organization's main goal?

What are the advantages and highlights of your items or

administrations?

What do your clients and prospects as of now think about your organization?

What characteristics do you need them to connect with your organization?

Do your exploration. Take in the necessities, propensities, and wants of your present and imminent clients. Also, don't depend on what you think they think. Realize what they think.

Since characterizing your brand and building up a brand methodology can be perplexing, think about utilizing the ability of a philanthropic independent venture warning gathering or a Small Business Development Center.

Once you've characterized your brand, how would you get the word out? Here are a couple of basic, time-tried tips:

1 **Get an awesome logo**: Place it all around.

2 **Write down your brand informing**: What are the key messages you need to impart to your brand? Each representative ought to know about your brand characteristics.

3 **Integrate your brand**: Branding reaches out to each part of your business- - how you answer your telephones, what you or your

salesmen wear on deals calls, your email signature, everything.

4 **Create a "voice" for your organization that mirrors your brand:** This voice ought to be connected to all composed correspondence and fused in the visual symbolism of all materials, on the web and off. Is your brand cordial? Be conversational. Is it luxurious? Be more formal. You get the substance.

5 **Develop a slogan**: Write an important, significant and brief explanation that catches the embodiment of your brand.

6 **Design layouts and make brand gauges for your advertising materials**: Use a similar shading plan, logo situation, look and feel all through. You shouldn't be extravagant, simply predictable.

7 **Be consistent with your brand**: Customers won't come back to you- - or allude you to another person - in the event that you don't convey on your brand guarantee.

8 **Be consistent**: I put this point last simply because it includes the majority of the above and is the essential tip I can give you. In the event that you can't do this, your endeavour at setting up a brand will fizzle.

19

(STEP FOUR)

PRICING:

HOW MUCH WILL YOU CHARGE YOUR CUSTOMERS?

There is no one size-fits-all answer for how to price products/services.

A successfully priced product/service typically requires the seller to:

1. Gain in-depth insight into how much a customer is willing to pay in order to solve the problem your solution intends to fix.

2. Consider competitors' pricing and how your solution compares.

3. Understand the relationship between quality and price.

QUANTIFY THE BENEFITS YOU'RE PROMISING:

When pricing something, it often helps to attempt to quantify in dollars and cents the real savings of your solution will offer your customers. This includes savings the customer may not consider at first glance. Some of these savings will be tangible allowing you to do research and assign a dollar amount to them. For example, the dollar amount of fuel savings if you buy a smaller car. Other savings might be more intangible (difficult to value). For example, the value of a full night's sleep or the value of your safety. Imagine you sold an organic frozen pizza that was 30% more expensive than non-organic frozen pizza. Although your option costs more upfront, consider the less-immediate (maybe less obvious) savings your pizza might offer to your customers.

1. Organic food retains more nutrients that lead to better health. How much money does the average person spend on doctor visits and medication a year?

2. If your pizza was packed with so many nutrients that the consumer wouldn't need to buy an extra vegetable that they regularly would buy otherwise, how much money would they save?

3. People who eat healthier tend to get more full nights of sleep. How much money is a full night of sleep worth to your customer?

MEASURE EVERYTHING!

If you experiment with pricing, measure how/if changes in price affected your sales metrics (ex: revenue, quantity sold, average order amount, order frequency, etc.) Measure your customers' savings

Channels: What Do You Use to Reach Your Customers?

A marketing channel is the way your product/service gets to the end-user. A marketing channel can serve the following purposes:

- Introduces your potential customers to your product/service
- Educates your potential customers on your product/service
- Enables your potential customers to purchase your product/service

Some examples of traditionally popular channels: direct sales, partnerships, magazines, franchises, web advertisements, social media, blogs, newsletters

20

(STEP FIVE)

GO TO WHERE YOUR CUSTOMERS ARE

With a thorough understanding of your target market, you can determine what channels will be most effective at reaching your specific potential customers. For example, if your target market are senior citizens then you might find that direct sales and partnerships with organizations like AARP will be more effective at reaching your intended audience than a social media platform like Snapchat.

CHANNEL PARTNER CONSIDERATIONS

Many startups find success through channel partnerships with other companies. Startups can use channel partners to help introduce, educate, and sell products/services. Channel partners care about their customers. This requires you to ask yourself how partnering with your company can benefit the channel partners' customers. When trying to identify partners, consider what products and services are sold before and after the purchase of your solution

INBOUND MARKETING

"Instead of the old outbound marketing methods of buying ads, buying email lists, and praying for leads, inbound marketing focuses on creating quality content that pulls people toward your company and product, where they naturally want to be." – HubSpot

Your audience is an asset that is a competitive advantage. When your startup utilizes social media to build a following, you are essentially renting the audience from the social media platform. For example, Facebook owns your followers. At any time, Facebook could change your relationship with your followers thus potentially making it more difficult for you to reach them. This doesn't mean don't use social media platforms. They can be very useful in helping you initially gain your following, but you should consider how you can eventually move the followers you gain over to a marketing platform that you have more control over. By producing unique content that your startup hosts on its blog, website, newsletter, etc., you can control your audience. The challenge is to produce truly unique and useful content that will draw new followers and (hopefully) eventually customers.

MEASURE EVERYTHING!

If you experiment with different channels, measure to see how/if different channels affected your sales metrics (ex: revenue, quantity sold, average order amount, order frequency, etc.)

21

(STEP SIX)

THE MARKETING & SALES CYCLE:

HOW DOES A LEAD BECOME A CUSTOMER?

THINK OF THE MARKETING & SALES CYCLE AS A FUNNEL

There are many different variations of how to depict this process, but most of them include similar concepts. At the top of the funnel are leads (potential customers). At the bottom are customers. The goal is to get the lead into the funnel and move them through the various stages as efficiently as possible until they come out at the end of the process as a customer.

QUALIFY LEADS EARLY AND OFTEN

Don't spend resources on leads that likely won't become customers. Qualify stronger leads early in the process so the least amount of resources is spent on weaker leads. Qualify leads often because things are always changing. As time progresses, strong leads can become weaker and weak leads can become stronger.

THE STAGES OF THE CYCLE

Awareness – at this stage you want to make your leads aware of your solution. This might also be time when a lead becomes aware of their problem. No matter how effective of a solution is being offered, this stage is usually one of the most difficult hurdles for a startup.

Interest – at this stage your goal is to convert a lead's awareness of your solution into interest in learning more about your product as a potential solution to their problem.

Education – at this stage you want to educate an interested lead on how your solution can fix their problem. Note that at this stage you are still not pushing them into a purchasing decision.

Engagement – at this stage your goal is to engage educated leads by showing them how to purchase your solution. This is the stage when you can begin to apply appropriate pressure to convince the lead to make a buying decision.

Trial – in some sales processes, but not all, leads may be offered a trial of your solution for them to test it out before they want to make the full purchase.

Purchase – this is when a lead purchases your full solution and becomes a customer. Taking a Lead from Awareness to Purchase Likely Won't Happen Overnight. More than ever, potential customers have the ability and willingness to research multiple options before making a buying decision. Depending on the industry, a sales cycle's duration can range from a matter of days to a matter of years.

UNDERSTAND WHAT THE SELLER CONTROLS VS WHAT THE BUYER CONTROLS.

As a seller, your business can control:

- The product/service and its features.
- The channels you use to generate leads.
- The resources you put toward moving leads through the sales process.

- The tools and methods you use to educate and engage leads.
- The customer retention efforts.

As a buyer, leads can control:

- The interest in your solution and the value they assign to solving their problem.
- The resources they have available to buy and implement your solution
- The resources they are willing to expend in order to get your solution
- The duration of the sales process.

WHO IS THE DECISION MAKER AT EACH STAGE?

Identifying the Decision Makers

In business-to-business (B2B) sales you need to identify the decision makers. Below are steps to identifying the decision makers.

AVOID STALLING THE PROCESS

Avoid the situation in which a lead wants to move forward in the sales process and you haven't provided them the necessary resources, incentives, and/or instructions to do so. To avoid stalling, continually communicate with your leads.

DO NOT ATTEMPT TO FORCE A LEAD THROUGH THE

SALES PROCESS

If a lead isn't ready to purchase and you apply too much pressure, you may risk irritating them enough that they won't consider you in the future. Converting a lead who isn't a good fit into an unhappy customer can backfire. Unsatisfied customers can be vocal and scare away future potential leads.

NOTE Unsatisfied customers can unnecessarily drain your resources and sanity.

Become more acquainted with Competition

You can take in a great deal about how to showcase and not advertise your item by investigating what the opposition is doing. In the event that there isn't an indistinguishable item available, at that point utilize comparable items as a component of your examination venture. Put on your buyer cap while doing your examination, see the item and contrast it and your own item from the perspective of the client. Adopting this strategy can enable you to pick up an understanding of what strategies may work to offer your item and what may not be as fruitful while thinking about the client.

22

(STEP 7)

LAUNCHING:

HOW DO YOU FIRST TELL PEOPLE YOU EXIST?

A launch is a public announcement that secures widespread attention while broadcasting your value proposition in order to drive a surge in demand for your product/service

Elements of a Great Launch

Timing – anticipate events happening in your industry, target market, and/or pop culture and attempt to tie or align your launch to those events

Influencers/Beta Customers – secure influencers and reference customers well before your launch date. Coach them on how to best represent your company.

Exclusive Content Offering – if possible, find one or a few media outlets and provide them exclusive content that is substantive and thoughtful. Media outlets value opportunities to give their viewers unique content

Consistent Messaging – Ensure all messaging, whether generated by your company or by a third party, captures the same key points.

Show, don't tell – Consider providing a video demo that can be shared

All Team Readiness – make sure all employees (regardless of roles) has the tools, coaching, and knowledge they need in order to answer questions

Make Mix of Marketing

Otherwise called the showcasing blend, to achieve your objective market, utilize diverse types of promoting, publicizing and media to contact them. Individuals from your objective market not just go on the web or read the nearby daily paper. Make sense of the diverse roads you can take to be the place your objective market is and afterward add it to your showcasing blend. Utilize some on the web, some up close and personal and some print types of advertising and track the reaction rates and consequences of each. Those with high reaction rates ought to be used once more. Those with not as much as ideal outcomes ought to be adjusted to enhance the reaction.

Make Buzz

Propelling the new item ought to include making a lot of buzz around the item dispatch. Use however many advertising strategies as could be expected under the circumstances to create mindfulness and accumulate enthusiasm for the item. A few organizations begin to make the buzz in the weeks paving the way to the huge dispatch. A progression of messages may go out to existing organizations saying things, for example, "We have energizing news to impart to you! On February 12, we'll be propelling an item that may change the way you do clothing. Stay tuned!" A consequent email may state, "Our huge news is only three days away. Is it true that you are prepared to reform your pantry? We are and we have exactly what you have to get it going. Stamp your logbook for February 12."

23

(STEP EIGHT)

CUSTOMER SUCCESS:

HOW DO YOU KEEP YOUR

CUSTOMERS HAPPY?

The Sales Cycle Shouldn't End with the "Purchase"

Customer retention should be an ongoing stage in your marketing & sales cycle. If the customer has already purchased from you, the process through the sales cycle should take less time and effort than it did when they were a new lead.

HOW TO GET CUSTOMERS TO KEEP COMING BACK, STAY LONGER, AND/OR PAY MORE

Your products/services have to continually help your customers achieve their desired outcomes. A customer's needs can change overtime. You need to understand their changing needs and be able to provide solutions through your products/services. It costs up to 5 times as much to attract a new customer then to keep an existing one. Not only is it cheaper to keep a new customer than it is find a new one, existing customers are also more likely to buy from you again and can be some of your most effective marketers. Companies that receive recurring revenue by charging customers periodic subscription fees, such as Software as a Service (SAAS) companies, recognize the vast majority of their income long after the initial onboarding of a customer Churn Rate – the annual percentage rate at which customers stop subscribing to a service. Keeping the churn rate low is vitally important to SAAS companies

THE BOTTOM LINE

To become a successful entrepreneur, you need to have certain qualities. You can develop these qualities if you are willing to open your mind and learn. Here are some practical guidelines to help you to become successful in business. Please don't quit your job and start your business full-time unless of course you have saved enough money to see you through the months.

There are many great business opportunities where you can start part-time without having to quit your job. Another reason for not quitting your job is new businesses need time to see real results. You need to allocate time to work on your business before it can generate income for you.

A successful entrepreneur is simply a person who has learned from someone successful who is doing what they want to do. But as always the challenge is being willing to stay the course when things get difficult.

Anyone who has ever thought about going into business for themselves have heard about the over 90% failure rate which is yet a reality. The road to success is littered with people who wanted to become entrepreneurs but who were unwilling to do everything it took to get there.

If you look at most of the stories of those who made it, you very rarely hear about how in five months starting from scratch they were making gobs of money and their business was taking off. Many of them, started from humble beginnings, worked hard all their life, with many setbacks before they found success.

So before you start assessing your options and trying to figure out what type of business you want to get involved with, what you want to start or invent, make sure you have the internal fortitude, sticking power and financial ware with all to become that successful entrepreneur that you say you want to be.

Successful people are those who know how to organize a business venture and assumes the risk for it, having made detailed plans of what they're doing for the next year. They continually measure how they're doing against the plan so they can make adjustments along the way.

These professional have mad passion for what they do. Take a look at any successful entrepreneur and consider how you would rate their passion for their product, business and life. Successful entrepreneurs have an almost infectious passion for things that drives them forward, inspire them to achieve greatness and keep them motivated when others would give up and take the easy route to a pay check.

There never seems to be enough time to do everything that you want to do, and you're performing several people's jobs at once, working evenings, weekends and public holidays to make sure that your business thrives or at least survives its first 12 months.

Do you have this amount of commitment in you? Self-belief: there will be times in any successful entrepreneur's career when their belief is tested. People will tell you that it cannot be done, that the idea just will not work, that it is folly to pursue such a dream. A real entrepreneur is one who is able to block out the doubters with their belief intact and stay the course.

Although entrepreneurship was once seen as the choice for people who did not have a career path, the fall of the economy and many more issues have people all over the world considering whether or not it is the path for them. While these issues can cause the path of an entrepreneur to be a rocky one, it is possible to become successful. What traits do the successful entrepreneurs share? Well let's take a look.

Be Grounded

Many may view the successful entrepreneur as an eccentric and strange person who is "off to himself," but the truth is that he is often a very grounded person. For example, if most people were to suddenly inherit a great deal of money, they would lose touch with reality for a bit and likely make several bad choices. For the successful entrepreneur, however, the possibility of gaining a lot of money all at once is a good once, but he or she also knows that money could be lost just as quickly. The successful entrepreneur has literally pulled himself up from the bottom, and knows how easy it is to fall back down. For that and more reasons, they are often more grounded than many would believe.

Be Self-Disciplined

While you may think that working for yourself would be the fairytale career, with no one to answer to, it requires a great deal of self-discipline to pull it off. Since there is no boss, no fear of being fired, and no time clock, there is often a temptation to have no responsibility. All too often, those who work for themselves tend to put things off until the last minute, and end up rushing the job. This is because many entrepreneurs find themselves taking off for a special occasion, or just because they don't feel well. Maybe they even take off for the weekend to spend time with the family. Whatever the case may be, the entrepreneur can often find it easy to put off going back to work. Monday turns into Tuesday, and suddenly the week is almost over and there is a whole week's worth of work to do. A great deal of self-discipline is required to stay on track and work the hours that you need to work.

Learn More Than One Skill

Because the successful entrepreneur often has to start their own business all by themselves, they will need to know how to operate every aspect of that business. In order to keep start-up costs low in an economy where funding may be impossible to get, many entrepreneurs put off hiring anyone until the business has already taken off. With that in mind, it is a good idea to learn many skills. Networking and marketing skills to run your own ad campaign, typing, and some computer skills in order to create your own website, business cards, logo, etc, and many more talents can be very helpful in making your venture a success. My motto is don't ask people to do a task you can't perform yourself. You hire employees to do work that you don't have time to do, not to do work that you don't know how to do. How should you be able to monitor the quality of the work your employees are doing if you don't even know how to do it yourself. This will separate the sucesfful CEO's from the failing ones.

Be Different

In 1997, Steve Jobs took over as the CEO of Apple Inc with a brand new slogan, "Think Different." As many know, he became one of the most successful entrepreneurs in the entire world. In order to be a successful entrepreneur, you must be able to think for yourself and step outside of conventional boundaries. He knows that by following everyone else, he will just end up where they are. The successful entrepreneur will dare to be different and cut the trail that everyone else will follow

Some who read this book will not change their attitude and will take my words lightly but for those who are truly inspired to go out there and break a leg in the business world I say go in charging like a bull plowing the path to your success. The failures will pile up quickly, the light at the end of the tunnel will get dimmer but don't let that hinder your indefatigable drive to achieve you end goal. No one accomplishes anything without failing first. You must never give up. The minute you give up is the minute you fail indefinitely. There is no such thing as luck. Everything has a equal and opposite reaction. If you work hard then your business will succeed. If you give up then your business will give up. If someone says, "you got lucky" then they are a loser. Luck is a mere illusion. People say, "you got lucky" because they don't want to credit your success. Don't ever let anyone discredit what you have built. You are the master of your future. You're the captian of your fate. You are the only factor in your own success and don't let anyone tell you otherwise. You must thank the people that helped you get where you are but you also must thank the people that doubted you. Anyone who doubts you is helping you because they are giving you reason to work harder and prove them wrong. The losers will always lose and the winners will always win because there is a fine line between failure and success. That fine line is known as effort and if you're not in it to win it then don't waste your time. 100% of people who read this book will fail but only 1% will try again. My hope is that after reading this you will change and improve so you too can succeed. Life is ten percent what happens to you and ninety percent how you react to it.

www.ingramcontent.com/pod-product-compliance
Lightning Source LLC
Chambersburg PA
CBHW070246230526

45470CB00002B/493